Reclaiming Humanity

Reclaiming Humanity

Revolutionary Pathways to Beloved Community

By Beth Roy

BLOOMSBURY ACADEMIC
NEW YORK · LONDON · OXFORD · NEW DELHI · SYDNEY

BLOOMSBURY ACADEMIC
Bloomsbury Publishing Inc, 1385 Broadway, New York, NY 10018, USA
Bloomsbury Publishing Plc, 50 Bedford Square, London, WC1B 3DP, UK
Bloomsbury Publishing Ireland, 29 Earlsfort Terrace, Dublin 2, D02 AY28, Ireland

BLOOMSBURY, BLOOMSBURY ACADEMIC and the Diana logo are
trademarks of Bloomsbury Publishing Plc

First published in the United States of America 2026

Published in cooperation with the Association for Conflict Resolution

Library of Congress Cataloging-in-Publication Data

ISBN: HB: 979-8-21637-477-0
PB: 979-8-21637-478-7
ePDF: 979-8-21637-480-0
eBook: 979-8-21637-479-4

Typeset by Deanta Global Publishing Services, Chennai, India

For product safety related questions contact productsafety@bloomsbury.com.

To find out more about our authors and books visit www.bloomsbury.com and sign up for our newsletters.

Contents

Acknowledgments

I may get the credit for writing this book, but in reality, like everything else I've ever written, it is a work of collaboration involving many others. As I began the project during the Covid-19 pandemic, I did not expect to be writing about the installation of an American leadership with intentions to kill every effort of recent years to bend US society toward justice. I thought I'd be writing an informative book about politics and psychology, but in the event the work became an act of political outcry as well as helping to preserve my own sanity. Both goals depended heavily on the support and contributions of many people.

For many years, Beverlee Pattonallen, Mary Adams Trujillo, and Mariah Breeding, deep friends and fellow authors, shared with me regular conversations about the pain and promise of writing. When some of us, with flagging will and compelling distractions, fell away for a time from the practice of putting words on paper, we renamed our little cohort an intentions group, and we enveloped in our dialogue everything from questions of health to relationships to politics to—yes, sometimes how to make order out of the chaos of half a dozen false starts to my particular project. Without these three, there would be no book. How blessed I am to have them in my life!

Also in a continuous stream of conversation about life and ideas and politics and faith, my friend and colleague Roberto Chené always thickens my analyses and widens my perspective, even as we share rage about oppressive systems. Every day, my digital devices hum with links to things Roberto recommends reading. Every few weeks, we share a meal at the café up the street and dominate a table with hours of conversation. Roberto is a large part of the reason we now live in New Mexico—so many reasons to be grateful to him!

Along the winding path through multiple drafts of the book, several different readers gave me invaluable thoughts and critiques. To learn from those I've taught is a particular kind of privilege. André Vaughn-Bonterre and Ripple (Tom) Krenning, both students of conflict transformation and coaching, read drafts and responded with enthusiasm and insight. Their thoughts are woven into many sections throughout the book.

So, too, I'm indebted to SY, whose personal verve, honesty, and history frame the book; more than once, SY has so generously served as my guide through thickets of racism and injustice.

My special thanks to all the individuals who grace these pages with their presence: George, Eladio, Lucy, Mia, Adi, two children in a grocery store and their moms, and many more. I'm both moved and very grateful for their generosity in allowing me to filter their stories through my lens and use them to illustrate theory.

This project is not the first time I've had the good fortune to work in dialogue with Hasshan Batts, always an experience that deepens my understanding of racism in worlds to which I have little access and in which he is a leader, advocate, and teacher.

At the next-to-last stage of the writing, I craved developmental editing, a process in which someone with a skilled eye looks over the work in detail and advises an author how to make improvements. I appealed to two dear friends, Michele Eodice and Kami Day, both writers, teachers of writing, and keen political minds, to provide that service. Now, I add to my gratitude for their friendship my thanks for exactly the reflections I needed to complete this book, everything from recognition and support for my intention to questioning awkward sentences and misplaced words.

One other constant companion on the journey through this writing was my brother, Rick Rapfogel. Rick assigned himself the role of copyeditor, correcting many drafts of this and other shorter manuscripts. He is also a masterful photographer; his images appear on the covers of several of my published books. What a special gift to have an editor, co-conspirator in political critique, and gifted image-maker, all rolled into one great brother!

And finally, Mariah, my partner of over thirty years: how many conversations about news and views over breakfast as well as suffering together through the endless evening search for good TV while enjoying arch critiques of the bad stuff. She both shares my thinking and challenges it, calling out dimensions I might otherwise hurry past or miss altogether. She kindly supports my obsessive absences, as I pound away at my computer in one room while in another, I know she is giving wise counsel to her clients about everything from the daily news to how to care for an ailing dog and what gives meaning to life in times of untenable duress and unjust oppression. Just as she makes sense of the senseless for them, she brings meaning and spirit into my life, contributions beyond gratitude.

All of this rich collaboration would in the end produce a limited product if it weren't for the efforts of three colleagues in the conflict intervention world: Cheryl Jamison, Michael Lang, and Susan Terry, founders and editors of the ACR Practitioner's Guide Series. Cheryl in particular gave me important editorial feedback as well as support early in the writing process. Beyond the enormous contribution of the literature they midwife into print, I thank all three of them for their leadership in crafting a profession that tries to live principles of equity and justice.

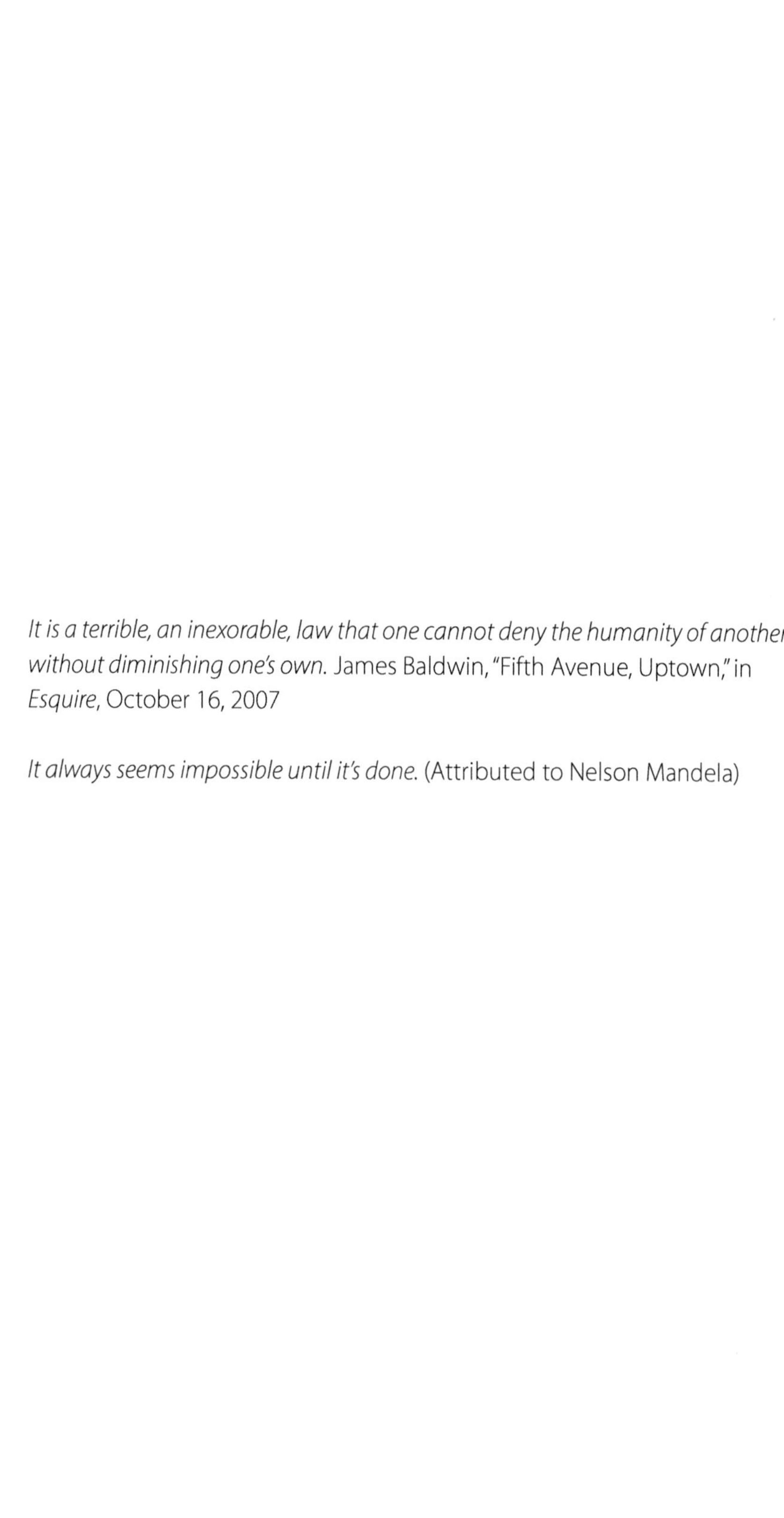

It is a terrible, an inexorable, law that one cannot deny the humanity of another without diminishing one's own. James Baldwin, "Fifth Avenue, Uptown," in *Esquire*, October 16, 2007

It always seems impossible until it's done. (Attributed to Nelson Mandela)

Introduction

Divisions at the Junction of Self and Society

If you're open to the challenge of questions that pierce to the heart of the matter, meet my friend SY.

"Why are white people still so racist?" she suddenly asked one day. "I mean, we've done so much work on that, we've learned so much, taught so much: how come so little has changed?"

A damn good question, I thought. When I was very young, I constantly challenged my elders with a child's version of the matter. How can people be so cruel, I insisted when I first learned about the massacre of our relatives in Europe? Why are *you* so unfair, I complained when I saw my parents deny a beloved Black domestic worker in our household something she really wanted. In so many instances, it seemed obvious to me that people could be kind, generous, honest—all the qualities I was told I was supposed to be. Why weren't *they*? "It's just the way the world is," I was told. "When you get older, you'll understand. You won't be so troubled."

Well, I'm in my ninth decade of life now; I'm still waiting to get old enough to understand. Toward that end, I'm writing this book, as explanation but, even more, as inquiry. I'm trained as a sociologist, but don't expect hard science within these pages. If reclaiming humanity is the question, then answers live in human experience, expressed in stories and the wisdom of friends. This book is unapologetically subjective, witness SY's story.

A middle-aged practitioner of the arts of restorative justice and mediation, SY has a unique talent for seeing and appreciating the humanity of people across all kinds of differences and divisions. She grew up in the projects in Harlem, New York, the youngest of a large bunch of siblings and cousins in an intensely entwined African American family. In elementary school, she was bused away to the posh Upper West Side of Manhattan, one of a handful of Black students "integrating" an otherwise all-white school. University and law school followed, more of the desegregation program of the times. Once graduated, SY took her first job in a firm staffed with white lawyers. Ushered before her as she sat in her new office behind her big shiny desk, her first clients ran out the story of their legal woes. She took careful notes and nodded with sympathetic understanding. When they came to the end of their account, they sat back and said, "Thank you so much for listening. When do we get to see the lawyer?"

On the spot, SY decided the job was not for her. How was she to work her legal and empathic magic if clients couldn't recognize her humanity? Instead, she became one of the pioneers of restorative justice in the juvenile justice system of her community.

I take SY's question very seriously. For all the impact of civil rights movements from abolition to voting rights, affirmative action, and DEI, the answer, I believe, lies somewhere deeper and less visible. Racism both causes and is caused by a pervasive alienation from a fundamental truth about the human condition: however different we are from each other—and we are poster children for natural variation—the greater reality is that we are all very much alike. But we lose a deep-seated sense of common humanity, rent apart by daily experiences of denial and deprivation. Oppression and malaise permeate advanced capitalist societies today, impacting people of all identities, for some communities in specific ways and across all identities in very universal ones. If you've ever lived with someone in pain, you probably know how difficult it is for a suffering person to maintain goodwill toward others. In a community where so many of us, separately and mostly silently, suffer insecurity, self-doubt, loneliness, or other manifestations of social dysfunction, it's no wonder that ill will and discrimination result. When my humanity is denied, I dehumanize others.

To take seriously SY's question, therefore, is to delve deeply into what's wrong with America and other modern societies. In writing from multiple perspectives—formal research, stories from my clients, the life I've lived—I mean to look at how we come to dehumanize others, and how we lose our own humanity in the process. To begin with such a broad question, I believe, enables us to explore the deep and structural problems that show up as all kinds of injustices, located in race, disability, gender, sexuality, and more. How does life need to be enriched for everyone? Nothing less stands a chance of breaching the painful social divisions that afflict us in a meaningful way: witness the paucity of change despite all the DEI programs, civil rights legislation, school desegregation, and more.

Racism is a particular source of pain to me. I am a child of the Holocaust and Jim Crow segregation. Those two realities of my youth combined to make me an early activist for racial change. I am also the mother and grandmother of a offspring of color. But this is not a book about bad white people and victimized people of color. It is a portrait of the ways we all become divided not only from each other but from our own ethical core, how in that process we accept lives of discontent, believe lies about necessary evils, and concede the inevitability of loneliness and insecurity. Breaches of integrity open pathways for opportunistic leaders who further our divisions and fail to satisfy our needs. I tell a story of moral dissonance, of white Americans who find ourselves inducted into complicity in systems of injustice that we abhor, of Americans of color who try but fail to fathom how racism can persist so stubbornly despite well-intentioned efforts to overcome it.

For all these ills, I seek also to paint a landscape rich in hues of change and creativity and resilience, of people overcoming manipulation and misinformation to build new cultures of solidarity. My underlying theory is that progress for any one group of people cannot be made without progress for everyone. White people in America are beset by deep and pervasive problems that go largely unaddressed. The absence of acknowledgment, of even a language in which to talk about these problems, fuels a turn toward demonizing those we think of as different but who in reality, just like us, suffer their version of the prevailing distress. When it comes to hardships, we're all one. We can't pick a single problem out of a barrel filled with problems. When an individual's troubles lie in a collective reality, then the solutions are collective. It's all or nothing.

I write from a very particular vantage point. I am a white, Jewish, lesbian, 85-year-old sociologist, mediator, therapist, grandmother, mother, wife, privileged member of the intellectual elite. An early marriage at twenty to a man from India immersed me in the lived experience of hateful exclusion. Nowadays, I care for a beloved partner of more than three decades who is disabled, living daily with pain, struggling resourcefully to overcome incapacity. Each of these aspects of who I am endows me with a particular standpoint from which I view the world. Each also could trap me in a limited view of reality, something I've spent a lifetime trying to escape. From all that I've done and learned, assumed and with surprise been challenged to revise, I offer a different way to understand the impact of inequality on us all. Because I believe we all have expertise to share based on the particularities of our lived experience, I draw in this book on a long lifetime lived in two locations: the United States and India. Although my personal stories are therefore grounded in unique features of those places, I try to extract principles and dynamics applicable everywhere: how we come to know who we are, and also how we are inducted into a kind of amnesia, forgetting that things we learned are not natural and inevitable. In fact, my bi-national experience serves me well in reminding me again and again to question normalcy and to imagine the ideal.

How Systems Endure . . . and How They Break

SY's anguished query focused on a particular ill of American life, the unjust consequences of racism for people of color. The persistence of racism is undeniably a bedeviling fact of life, a bedrock feature of life that demonstrates in many ways how social wrongs become normalized and intractable. So much is known about prejudice, implicit bias, institutional exclusions, and other facets of the problem. Schools have been integrated, redlining of neighborhoods outlawed, protections enacted against employment discrimination. Corporations hire DEI experts and mediators who offer workshops and interventions. And yet every day, people of color are mistreated by cops, judged less qualified to be hired for jobs, denied admission to universities, subjected to "microaggressions," and more, while other people, those not directly impacted, fail to witness and therefore tacitly collude with these discriminatory practices.

We understand how certain interpersonal transactions convey racism. Many studies reveal the continuation of systemic disadvantages. Recent books by authors like Ta-Nehisi Coates, Isabel Wilkerson, and others eloquently describe one or another dynamic, drawing links and connections. And yet, change eludes us. Is it simply a matter of white people protecting privilege, a manifestation of selfishness and other moral failures? Or that people of African descent, Latinos, Native Americans, and others have been kept so hopelessly behind that "catching up" is an impossibility?

My answer to questions like these involves a belief that social systems have a life course and ours in America is at a breaking point. Strains like racism reflect the ways the system was never adequate to meet human needs. Similarly, unsustainable rates of "mental illness" combine with unattended needs of poor people and even of the middle class to shout out the failures of modern capitalism. But capitalism bends and twists, providing just enough to keep people in thrall to compelling and confusing myths that serve to protect itself. I put this in an impersonal voice because no cabal of billionaires sits in a bunker somewhere plotting how to keep on top of society. Instead, the maintenance of an unmaintainable system happens in many different rooms, through many decisions, and even more, through impersonal dynamics of exchange and repression.

Earlier social systems similarly lasted for centuries, despite misery, oppression, and injustice. But eventually, change happens. New means of producing the things people need arise, and with them, new means of exchange and new demands on how daily life is organized. Do people live in cities or on the land? In multi-generational households or in nuclear families? Do the sun and the seasons mark the hours of the day, or does industrial time rule the clock? Does the family work together to make crafts at home, or do the adults commute long distances to labor on an assembly line in a huge industrial factory? Eventually, the imperative need for these forms of social reorganization breaks through sociopolitical structures that restrain needed changes. People rebel; new social forms are created. I write in a time when modern capitalism has reached such a point. The autocratic regime in power in the United States right now disrupts norms and assumptions, rending the normalcy of daily political functions, opening pathways to dictatorship and fascism, but also to rebellion and progressive social change. Sometimes, when things get worse, we come to know it's time to make them better.

But if the dynamics of social change are historic, the embodiment is human. There is a very old debate about whether history moves by its own laws along materialist tracks beyond the altering of human choice, or whether history is made by humans through choice and will. It may already be obvious that I believe both to be true. We need to understand dynamics of identity, oppression, and containment of rebellion, those facets rooted in an individual perspective, at the same time we look at these same processes through an institutional lens. Ultimately, finding the means to remake society from one full of cruel flaws into one where equality, justice, and sustenance are everybody's birthright requires clarity about how personal and systemic viewpoints intertwine.

Who's Crazy Here?

Inequality is the inescapable fault line in capitalism and discrimination—racism and all the other "isms"—the harbinger of unsustainability: the canary in the mine. But the song emanating from the canary's cage is mostly overwhelmed by other noise. How modern cultures conceptualize mental illness is one key dynamic that distracts attention from the truth of the matter, a sub-sonic hum that normalizes deprivation suffered by masses of people of all races and diverts attention to competition for resources. What gets commonly defined in psychiatric terms I think of as manifestation of alienation. Depression, anxiety, failure to sustain viable relationships, isolation from community: all these epidemic symptoms of a troubled social order that are talked about as individual problems actually flow from socioeconomic realities that deprive us all of the rich lives we deserve. There are links between the persistence of obstacles specific to people of color and others who share vulnerable identities, and the widespread failure to thrive of millions of Americans who are white. Fighting racism is therefore a matter of mutuality, not something that people of color must combat alone, not something that well-meaning white people might do for others. We all live in a social system and a culture that undermines the ability of each of us to live life to the fullest, to dwell in creativity, and to enjoy those human connections that sustain well-being.

My work as a counselor, mediator, and scholar of conflict over many decades focuses my attention on the spot where the personal and the political coincide. Compounding cultural factors obscure clear vision of how much traits like personality, identity, worldview, and character are at root manifestations of social conditions. That obscurity renders invisible dynamic understandings that go beyond the intractability of racism. It also makes it difficult for white people to understand how we ourselves are harmed. We may deplore injustices done to others, but we miss the damages we too incur. People seek psychotherapy for conditions that experts tell us are about our biology and "treat" with chemicals. Depression and anxiety plague sufferers who blame deficits in themselves and accept professional interventions that medicate symptoms but do little to remedy underlying deprivations. "Patients" complain of loneliness, inability to sustain relationships, family life tortured by conflict, jobs without meaning and without exit that induce leaden spirits and despair. Each of these experiences, individualized, reinforces isolation, producing unhappiness that the currently fashionable psychiatric medication (promoted by a multibillion-dollar pharmaceutical company) cannot effectively relieve.

My aim is to lay out these dynamics in detail, running out the ways emotional and institutional realities reinvent and reinforce each other and in the process lock in dehumanization, of others and also of ourselves. Starting with the formation of identity, the way we recognize ourselves in relationship to a universe of social groupings, I show how a sense of self becomes laced with consent to inequality and injustice. I trace the personal parts of these processes to ways we construct knowledge, the types of experience we draw on to form mental maps of our world. Knowledge is not impartial; it comes to us laden with instructions in power, place, and acceptable behavior. How ideology bonds with identity underwrites the sustainability of "isms." Not least among the ways we are crafted to accept inequities and unhappiness are the ways we learn to construct thought itself: categorically, linearly, abstractly. All these factors—how we think, what we think about, what we *don't* recognize or think about, and how we share all that with others—result both in increasingly polarized social divisions and increasingly prevalent individual malaise.

But if we're all harmed, what becomes of the responsibility for those of us who enjoy certain privileges to those who do not? This aspect of the matter is often talked about as "accountability," a word I find problematic. What I know from my conflict and counseling work is that people rarely change attitudes or behaviors because of guilt-inducing judgment. Finger-pointing more often results in stubborn resistance. Yes, there are actions that those of us who benefit as participants in dominant power relations can and should take: to learn what we need to know in order to be conscious of how things we do harmfully impact others, for one example among many. We are more likely to be open to that recognition and those changes, however, if we are motivated by both self-interest and love rather than by judgment. But we cannot love those who lie beyond a false dividing line created by every institution and many cultural tropes we encounter every minute of every day. So there's a circular problem: severely divided, if we who are white, or able-bodied, upper class, or male, or whatever category of advantage we occupy, do not know what we need to know; if further we feel resentful when charged with failing to be accountable; if we are frightened, baffled, guilty, and unwilling to reach across barriers to find the needed learning, then we are all locked into an untenable status quo. But if we first recognize that our own lives will be bettered right along with contributing to relief from oppression for people on the disadvantaged side of the line, then the need and the willingness to understand what oppresses us all increases and the hope of positive change grows greater. We are all caught in an unstable boat on a stormy sea. We can only survive—and maybe even enjoy the ride—if we regard all our fellow passengers as equally valued humans whose fates are joined inextricably with our own.

Putting the Pieces Together

In the pages that follow, I focus on three interlocking facets of modern life: individualism, psychiatry, and capitalism. None, I contend, can exist without the other two. All are laced with dynamics of inequality and therefore are complicit in the persistent malaise that propels so many of us onto the psychiatrist's couch. Individualism is often confused with individuality. *Individuality* refers to what is unique about each of us. It is about creativity, intelligence, personality, and more: all the wonderful variety among humans, what makes us different, what makes us special. *Individualism,* on the other hand, is an ideological system that divides each person from collectivities. It leaves us alone on an island responsible for our own well-being, our own choices of what's true or false, our own reality. By *psychiatry,* I do not mean the actual professionals who prescribe medication and charge big bucks. I mean the mental health industry, both the "services" it provides and also the ideology embodied in its core premises. *Capitalism* is a particular system of economic relations. What's most relevant to what I'm writing is its impact on social relations as it enforces hard lines of hierarchy and inequality. Lived from within its structures and belief system, capitalism seems inevitable, the best of all possible worlds. I strongly believe it is not. It is a system grounded in the value of money, the mechanism of competition, and the necessity of acquisitiveness. Nowhere in that trilogy lies the human heart and spirit, nor the love of nature without which none of us will long survive.

When people ask me what my book is about, I'm at a loss for one short answer. This book is about the reasons why after all these years of struggle, legislation, programs, and teachings about diversity, equity, and inclusion, this country in which I live is still so racist. Simultaneously, it is also about why the people who come to me for help with their personal problems, people of all races and identities who should be enjoying the very best that America has to offer, who live obedient lives and work responsible jobs, why these citizens of the land dedicated to the pursuit of happiness are so unhappy. My clients come seeking therapy because their marriages are broken, their friendships frayed, and their children addicted to drugs. They come to work on escaping their isolation, seeking help to build communities they cannot locate. They come for counsel about how to find meaning in their working lives. And they come needing intervention in conflicts with colleagues, loved ones, parents, and children that defeat respect and love and tear their families and hearts apart.

Through it all, this book is about the puzzle of why this land of equality allows an obscene inequality in the sharing of resources. How has it come to be true that the top one percent of American families own thirty percent of the wealth while so much of the population lives with financial insecurity and thirteen out of every hundred people are defined by the federal government as in poverty?[1] What can we understand by unpacking the stunning contradiction between the mythology of America, the land of equality, and these indisputable metrics of the stark opposite?

What to Expect

It is often helpful to have a roadmap to what lies ahead. Here's a little more detailed preview of the roads I take to explore these questions:

In Part I, I build a conceptual toolkit: Since modern social divisions are built on identity, I start by looking at how we form a sense of ourselves as individuals and as members of collectivities. I go on to explore the ways these identities become politicized as we internalize sets of rules and restrictions associated with them, defining our "place" in the social order. Right along with the rule book, we also internalize a limited conceptual toolkit with which to think about our lived experiences. In the industrialized and now digitized world, our ways of thinking tilt toward the scientistic; we analyze with metrics, see things in binaries, divide the world into static categories and simplify complex realities into linear lists that we can number and rank. And we end up mystified by harsh realities lived day by day. I relate all these elements to the appeal and hazards of religion, as solace but also as political enterprise.

Part II takes us directly to the use of the concepts from the first chapters to look at race, class, gender, and other social divisions. I argue that the distresses of middle-class white people need to be understood in the context of a social structure built on discrimination experienced by people of color and other challenged categories of people. Making concrete the vast inequalities of class in society makes it possible to see how and why all inequalities remain so durable, and how we all come to be complicit in the very social ills that afflict us.

And then we come to the point of the exercise: Part III is about social change: not surface reforms which inevitably fail to touch the problems as we live them, not DEI but system change. All meaningful progress, I believe, begins with a simple complaint, the first cry of almost every two-year-old: It's not fair! Only when we see our problems as the result of injustice rather than inadequacies in ourselves, of common injuries inflicted by a shared social reality rather than a competition for resources between contesting communities, can we begin to create the humane realities we crave. That, after all, was the point of SY's question. I knew she asked it not as accusation but, in anger and love, with deep hope.

Part I

Becoming Human in a Dehumanizing Culture

2 **Identity**

Who Am I? Who Are You? Where Do I Fit?

At about the age of ten months, Lucy was adopted from an orphanage in a country distant from her new parents' home. Staying their first night with her in a hotel room, her new mom and dad turned the crawling baby loose to explore her new surroundings. Soon she discovered a full-length mirror. Pulling herself to her feet, she touched the image of herself, then her own belly, then the glass again. Back and forth her hands wandered exploring, discovering, visibly constructing a concept of herself, and also of "not-self": a piece of the material world called a mirror.

"Myself": does a newborn have a sense of self? When did I recognize that I am separate from all others? How did the cord binding me to mother, sister, caregiver, pet dog finally spring loose, yielding recognition of my unique personhood? Can there be consciousness without consciousness of "myself," an entity different from all others around me?

These questions may seem existential—and unanswerable. I pose them for a particular purpose. Today's politics wind intricately through dynamics of identity. How you see yourself is not necessarily the same as how *I* see you. At a friend's wedding, in a crowd overwhelmingly composed of heterosexual couples, I intensely experience my identity as lesbian. The groom's brother, however, a nice young man I'm meeting for the first time, no doubt accounts me only old and female. Perceptions of others' identities change with the times and contexts: passers-by on a Manhattan sidewalk may one day have regarded a bearded, turban-wearing young man as a visitor from an exotic land, but on September 12, 2001, that same young man might have been feared as a dangerous terrorist. Did the police officers who stood by as their partner slowly choked the life from George Floyd see their victim's identity as anything other than Black? Did they equate that label with "not human" or "criminal" and so assume George Floyd did not need or deserve their protection?

Becoming "Myself" and Entering the World of Politics

Many years ago, I had the privilege as a researcher of talking deeply with people in very different parts of the world about these dynamics of identity and knowledge. The first was a case study of a communal riot in Bangladesh in the unpacking of which I tracked political aspirations expressed in terms of identity conflict.[1] My next project took the analytic framework developed in South Asia to Little Rock, Arkansas, where I interviewed people connected with the desegregation of Central High School at about the same historical moment that people in a far distant village fought it out in Bangladesh.[2] As rageful adults outside the all-white school sought to prevent the enrollment of nine Black youngsters, students inside went about their daily lives with relative disinterest in the uproar surrounding them. "I just went in the side door, went to my locker, no big deal," one middle-aged white woman told me, describing her young self. "It was just a way of life," said her friend. Witnessing daily harassment of their Black classmates, one white alumna after another told me, fifty years after the fact, that they chose not to get involved—or if history revealed they had indeed been involved, to portray themselves as the true victims of the drama.

Both these events—villagers in Bangladesh deciding collectively to reorganize political power in their village by rioting and white high school students in Little Rock choosing "neutrality" and proclaiming their own victimhood—are stories of the construction of identity and worldview. Identity describes a sense of self: who am I in the context of the world around me. Worldview contains beliefs about how that world works as well as values, a moral lexicon of assumptions about how the world *should* work. None of these processes takes place in isolation; the social structures within which we form a sense of self simultaneously impose hardships. Limitations of resources, emotional strains suffered by the people around us, force applied by institutional arrangements like isolated family life and overcrowded schools, injustices based in race, gender, disability, and other attributes, all these forms of oppression translate into learned beliefs about our own capabilities, rights, appropriateness, lovability, and more.

How then do these solidified identities become politicized? Each of us has many different identities. In a study of mixed-race people, Cathy Toshiro delineated five distinct dimensions to how each of us experiences identity: our own deep-felt sense of who we are; identities ascribed to us by others; cultural identity, meaning that sense of commonality connected with the things we love to eat and other aesthetic sensibilities; how we name ourselves in terms of race, class, gender and so on; and, perhaps most illuminating, situational identity: where we go in moments of perceived danger.[3] Moreover, we each occupy multiple identity categories, what is known as intersectionality. I've said I am both grandmother and professor; it's fairly obvious that I most experience one rather than the other of these identities when I'm associating with grandkids or with students. Often, we experience a given identity in the context of risk. I am aware of being an old woman when I walk down an urban street alone at night. On the other hand, standing at a lectern reading from my recently published book, I occupy the role and therefore the identity of intellectual. Also, submerged just beneath that sense of self I am aware of my white identity and how much it helped me become a published author, of my privilege.

Given a multiplicity of identity possibilities, why did the villagers in Bangladesh coalesce along a Hindu-Muslim axis rather than a tiller-landlord one? I believe that none of us acts entirely out of misguided understandings; there's always some kernel of reason to our choices. In the case of race in the United States, what's the mix of right and wrong in the assumptions and calculations we make? And how, taken altogether, do they result in the social divisions that so characterize modern America and much of the world?

As we grow toward adulthood, exploring the world we find ourselves in and ourselves in that world, we draw on the resources available. In my Bangladesh study, I proposed a schema for what those resources are. Like all simplifications of complex realities, this one is far from exhaustive, offering, however, some guidelines for understanding the formation of worldviews by looking at the realms in which we discover the knowledge we need:

- *Lived experience*: the many events we've personally encountered; Lucy at the mirror; for example. We figure out things both when we are alone and also, perhaps primarily, through interactions with others, some verbal and many others not. How do the complex social dynamics among children teach lessons in power and competitiveness, for example, especially among siblings but also among friends and classmates? What we make of this pool of learning, however, is filtered through our own senses, uninterpreted by others.

- *Discourse in community*: the "buzz" in our families, neighborhoods, schools, offices, and so on; what and how those around us think. These messages are as often emotional as verbal, expressed with intonation, body language, jokes and a million other forms of unnoticed human communication, all the more persuasive for being without words. They put language to what we've lived, sometimes directly but more often by association and innuendo.

- *Impersonal sources*: social media, books, popular culture, and so on. Everything we encounter in the public domain is curated to express and reinforce cultural norms. Nothing published, whether in digital or paper form, is without subtexts of power relations. This form of learning layers on direct experience and interpretations by others to situate knowledge in an explicitly social frame.

We come to know what we know and to explore what we don't through all our human faculties. How we think, the emotions we experience, our somatic sensations: all reflect the internalization of values and beliefs about who we are and how we're supposed to behave. To see how all these ways of knowing weave together, stories are a crucial source.

Recognizing Difference, Solidifying Separation

In 1951 I was ten, and my family moved from New York City to Fort Worth, Texas. Post–Second World War, there was a sense in the United States, perhaps in the world, of mobility. Moving for work, for safety, for liberation from oppressive conditions, seemed a reasonable option. Black southerners moved north. Survivors of the Holocaust moved to the Americas, north and south, and of course to Israel. Employees of increasingly huge and dominating corporations moved again and again and again to wherever they were posted. I'm not certain of the reasons why my parents decided to leave New York—I suspect it had something to do with inter-generational conflict combined with a desire for adventure, but the unlikely place they chose was Fort Worth, a medium-sized city in central Texas where the Jewish population numbered less than 1 percent.

In the suburban community where we'd lived in New York, my sister and I had experienced various examples of anti-Semitism, some subtle, others very overt. I remember eavesdropping on a grown-up conversation at our dining table late one night. Speaking just above a whisper, my parents leaned close to my uncle and aunt, tension clear to my six-year-old ear. The question they debated was whether my aunt should lie about her maiden name on job applications. They agreed with certainty that anti-Semitism accounted for her repeated rejections. Should she avoid admitting that her maiden name was "Goldberger," a clear indicator of her religious identity? Or would the lie be discovered and she somehow punished?

It was only a year after the end of the world war, and I knew about the Holocaust. How did I know? I'm certain no adult explicitly told me; indeed, I'm sure they did everything they could to protect us children from the news. But there were refugees staying with us from time to time: a distressed teenaged cousin, the only relative who got out of Europe in time; a tall Hungarian woman who had a psychotic break when my brother was born; and, most impactfully for me, a couple who lived in our basement and briefly worked for my family while "getting on their feet." When she wasn't dusting or ironing or doing other light domestic tasks, the woman sat on a chair by the furnace and wept. I stood beside her, leaning against her heaving shoulder, wanting desperately to comfort her. We shared no language, but she swept me wordlessly onto her lap, hugging me to her bony chest. I felt her heartbeat in rhythm with her sobs, and I wrote my own story of her tragedy. She had a little girl, just my age, who died in the Holocaust; the mother's grief was unrelenting. So too, I thought, would my mother grieve were I to die. How did I make connections between whatever forbidden images of concentration camp survivors I may have glimpsed before adults could hide them, and the flesh-and-blood, emotionally wrought people who walked briefly through our lives?

A few years later we drove south on our migration to Texas. At the first restaurant beyond the Mason-Dixon line we encountered a sign: "We reserve the right to refuse service."

"Could they refuse to serve us?" I puffed up my outrage feathers, ready to protest.

And so we learned about legal segregation. Such unfair discrimination racially imposed I knew to be wrong, whether inflicted on me or on others.

My sister and I, on the cusp of adolescence, soon found ourselves embedded in a small society of Jewish teens. My parents were not observant Jews; they belonged to no congregation in New York. But they promptly joined one of the two synagogues in Fort Worth, for the sake of community. Most of the few Jewish families lived in the same part of town we did, so we went to the same schools. As the years between ten and college went by, my social life was almost entirely bounded by those Jewish friendships. After the Supreme Court's ruling abolishing legal school segregation, my family spoke out courageously. My father had already integrated his medical practice, insisting that all hemorrhoids hurt alike. I joined a small committee of citizens bent on preparing the city to implement school desegregation (which didn't in fact happen for another fifteen years).

But while we campaigned for integration in one domain, we ourselves remained strictly segregated. There was no legal enforcement of religious or ethnic separation, but there might as well have been. I was unusual in having three non-Jewish friends, two of them Catholic, one Protestant, but I connected with them mostly at school, rarely in our free time. The Jewish pack of kids, on the other hand, hung out on weekends, often at our house. We went on expeditions together, held dances, indulged in cliques and intrigues, and generally did all the pack-like teen things kids did in those days.

One day recently, it occurred to me to question the mechanisms by which the social lines were so strictly drawn. No gentile schoolmate ever invited us to a birthday party; no Christian boy ever asked my sister or me to dance at a school event. If no invitation was extended on that side of the line, neither did any come from our side. While I assumed exclusion was imposed on us by anti-Semitism, I was now considering the idea that we participated as well. There was mutuality in our separation, if not equality.

How did we know to stay within our circle? We all got the memo, but who wrote it? I remember hateful warnings from my grandmother: "Scratch a gentile and you'll find an anti-Semite." But I wasn't frightened by these slogans, however ominous they were meant to be, nor by knowledge that there were people in the world who would kill me if they could, even though they didn't know me. When neighborhood boys in New York chased us at Easter time yelling, "Christ killers!" my sister hid but I ran to my father's office, unoccupied at the moment, grabbed a large hypodermic syringe with which I'd witnessed him removing water from some hapless patient's knee, and I chased those boys away. When *Brown v. Board of Education* was declared, I had no fear about speaking out for desegregation almost alone among my peers. Yet I too mostly kept to the rules of socializing within my group, my identity centered on "Jewish."

Years later, my young grandson taught me something about how messages, especially those conveying identity and the rules of the game, are sent, received, integrated, contested, and adopted.

Reaching Out with All Senses

At three, Adi is strapped into his child seat behind Shelby, a family friend who picks him up from pre-school several times a week. He feels safe with Shelby; she fulfills his physical and emotional needs, playing with him joyfully, hugging him frequently, showing up on a predictable schedule, joining in family dinners and special events. She is an integral part of Adi's life. Today, Adi and Shelby are silent as Shelby negotiates the crowded roads of the city. Out of nowhere, Adi asks, "Shelby, do you live alone?"

Surprised, Shelby replies, "Yes, I do."

A thoughtful pause, then, "I think I'd be sad to live alone. Are you sad?"

That's Adi weaving the pieces of his world together around a central concept of "self."

He lives with parents and a sister. Lots of other adults inhabit his world regularly—many friends, grandparents, cousins, and other kin. In his peopled world, he experiences, and at that moment in Shelby's car, names the absence of an emotion he has felt under other circumstances: sadness. He has pieced together the idea that Shelby (a) lives alone and (b) may therefore be sad in contrast to his absence of sadness. Another piece we can guess: (c) not everyone experiences identical emotional responses to things. *He* would be sad, but he acknowledges he doesn't really know whether *Shelby* is.

Aside from a grandmother's boasting about her empathic grandson, the complexity of that process boggles the mind. It involves inductive and deductive reasoning, intuition and empathy, inquiry, and love.

Adults don't lose the abilities Adi demonstrated. We, too, constantly construct and reconstruct knowledge. But the range of possible conclusions available to us constricts with time. Like a house of cards, changing one opinion shakes so many others. Someone in a dying marriage might think to herself, "Shelby must be lonely and sad. If she were not, then I might have to question the fear of loneliness that causes me to stay in this barren marriage of mine.

Is it possible that coupling is not the most perfect form of union? Could singleness truly be a happy option?" And so we cage certain perceptions, taming them within bars in order not to challenge the premises on which we've built our lives.

At three, Adi spoke his curiosity without constraint, not yet having learned that his question might be hurtful to Shelby. Had he kept a polite silence he might not have learned that Shelby was in fact content to live alone. Adi's lived experience denied him that knowledge: he lived with parents and sister. Had he ever in his three years actually been alone? Probably not. Knowing that others were, he could fill in the knowledge he missed relationally: by intuiting Shelby's experience, by asking the question, and by believing her answer. Of the ways we know the world, this ability to learn from others' knowledge is centrally important. We can ourselves live only narrow slices of all possible realities. But we can expand our understanding of the world by drawing on others. Which others? Primarily, we rely on those with whom we have some rapport. The connection may be familial or geographic, people we love or people we fear or people we respect or know others respect. These known associations combine in complex chemical reactions with knowledge gleaned from our own experience.

Adi drew on both these sources: lived experience and interpersonal associations. At three, he lacked a third pool from which we derive knowledge: impersonal sources such as media, books, popular culture, and other forms of distant information.

The model I've sketched here, of interaction between sources of knowing, is, like all models, an abstracted simplification of far more complex realities. Those beautiful miniature skyscrapers and bridges sitting in architects' offices bypass real-world problems and contradictions every engineer knows she will confront in the act of actual building. Nonetheless, I use the schema I've outlined here as the scaffolding on which to build this book. Everything we know is constructed in the context of our past experiences, under the influence of our present interactions, and shaped by our cultural assumptions. All that is anchored in material realities of economy and resources. There is a difference between things we do unmediated by interaction with others and things that we perceive and understand in ways inextricably interconnected with other people. The second category of experiences is by far the larger. Very rarely do we humans find ourselves in a new situation in which we perceive something fresh, with no context that provides directions for interpretation beyond our own prior experiences. I would posit that the possibility of such freshness expires in infancy. It is possible, for instance, that before Shelby, Adi had never encountered anyone whom he knew to live alone. To have formulated his question, however, he must have reviewed in his mind information he already had. I imagine him asking himself, who are the people Shelby lives with? He knew that I lived with Mariah, that Gabriela lived with Katherine, that Penny lived with a shifting cast of roommates. His question to Shelby represented his recognition of a null set: a category of lifestyle identified by the absence of a known living companion.

What was his route to formulating the question? It might have been pure observation of the difference I've defined here. But I suspect it was not. Since his next cognitive step was to associate living alone with an emotional state, sadness, I have a hunch it was the recognition of something emotional from which Adi worked backward. I imagine something like this:

An aura of sadness surrounded Shelby. A resourceful person, joyful in her core being, she was nonetheless challenged with a recurrence of a very serious cancer. Indeed, she had relocated to Adi's hometown in order to be present soon after his birth, to be part of his extended family, knowing her time on earth was limited. Nobody knew how long Shelby would live. She availed herself of every intervention, medical and alternative, available to her, and that determination had kept her alive longer than most people with her diagnosis.

But on a subterranean emotional level, we all lived in fear and sadness. Adi had no understanding of the conditions Shelby battled. Although we grownups had introduced the children to the word "cancer," we were careful to protect them from the full force of our emotions, wishing to relieve them of the emotional work of solacing us. But kids are keen observers of that which is not said; Adi no doubt picked up "sad" and cast about to understand a contradiction: Shelby evoked sadness, sometimes emitted it herself, and yet she was happy around Adi, playing with him boisterously, laughing and undeniably happy to be with him.

Emotional contradictions like this constitute powerful moments of learning. I think of them as cracks in the coherence of our worldviews. For children in particular, curiosity is a primary force. The less in control of the conditions of our lives we are, the more we need to understand what's going on in order to be able to negotiate whatever must be negotiated. If my reckoning of Adi's process is (mostly) correct, we can see that Adi is both right and wrong. Yes, Shelby is sad, but not because she lives alone. Or perhaps not only because she lives alone; there is a greater source of sadness that Adi does not (yet) have the needed knowledge to understand. So too adults get things both right and wrong, truth and distortion mixed together to form a stew of assumption and, sometimes, misdirection.

In the kind of counseling and mediation I practice, this concept of truth/not-truth is very central. Decades ago, colleagues who preceded me in the practice reclaimed the concept of paranoia, pronouncing it not insanity but keen intuition. In other words, we all constantly scan our environments from a perceptual place that is non-verbal. We *sense* the time of day. We *feel* tensions in the air. We *vibrate* with happiness when in the presence of another person's celebration. On a dark night walking down an unfamiliar street, our skin *tingles* with apprehension. All these experiences are largely somatic; none instantaneously involves an analytic or intellectual process. But in practice, it is not difficult to elicit the narratives we all concoct about other people's judgments, motivations, intentions, and so on. Whether they take the form of intuition or fear, analysis or theory, often our imaginings about others' realities direct our own behaviors and choices.

While Adi attended to the rich brew of both emotional information and direct communication from his adults, he was also busily interpreting what he picked up, fitting pieces together to make coherence. Like pieces of a jigsaw puzzle needed to make sense to him, given the framework of what he already understood. "Cancer" held little meaning, given our well-intentioned practice of protecting the children by stripping our own emotional intensity from the work. But "aloneness" evokes for a small child a complex context. When was Adi ever alone? At bedtime, when he still insisted on elaborate pre-sleep rituals: story reading, an adult sitting with him, rubbing his back, helping him slip into a sufficient sense of safety and calmness to fall asleep. Transitions from together to alone are fraught times for most children; an early project is to construct rituals of self-reassurance in order to navigate a state of being that is new to the newborn, fresh from the connectedness of the womb, and in many cultures never encountered until far later in life. Indeed, the practice of separating children from other humans at night is, I believe, part of the project of constructing individualism, a quality unique to the modern era.

Context is everything as we go about daily life, making sense of interactions and other experiences. Even minor occurrences—Lucy at the mirror, Adi conversing with Shelby on the car ride home from school—carry thick messages about identity, values, agency and where we fit in a social matrix of interlocking relationships, all of them deeply colored in hues of inequality. Very early in life in America, these elements of consciousness become interlaced with attitudes and assumptions embodying race, gender, class and other social locations.

3 Masculinity, Violence, and Racism

How Men Internalize Patriarchy

When we examine various discriminatory dynamics attached to identity, we tend to do so piecemeal. One activist group decries racism, another sexism, a third ableism or ageism. While each effort to advance equity may achieve a measure of success, each alone reaches a hard stop at some point. Sometimes coopted into the mainstream with small achievements to its credit, sometimes smashed with a heavy mallet as politics swing wildly to the right, separate causes swirl around and do not touch core matters of power.

At root, however, all forms of inequality and discrimination link to one single form of dominance, a fundamental structural feature of the vast majority of societies known to recorded history: patriarchy. Setting both mindset for dominance and its structural reality, the control of women by men intertwines with all other forms of enforced hierarchy, linkages I'll explore in this chapter and the next.

Whatever variations there are in particular forms of social organization, what all patriarchies have in common is that men sit above women in the hierarchy. Matriarchal cultures may still exist in a few aboriginal communities, but even they are subject to the controls and oppressions of the larger patriarchal forms with which they must contend. Contemporary capitalist societies uniformly manifest significant discriminatory differentials between genders, even while women's access to independence, both financial and reproductive, advances and stalls periodically. Even in the most advanced modern societies, even in places where women have occupied seats of political power, essential power still remains in the hands of men. Whether by metrics of wealth, control of key economic entities, politics, or whatever other measures one wishes to cite, women barely show up on the rosters of the functional power elite.

If men control the levers of social control, we need to look at how masculinity is constructed, and especially the ways that it supports the continuation of racism, sexism, and the other forms of inequality we decry.

The fundamental aspect of patriarchy is violence—sexual violence inflicted on women, suppressive violence toward men and women of color, violence in war that threatens all men everywhere. The very first act of violence inflicted by patriarchy—the action, I would say, that enables patriarchy to become implanted in every person's psyche—lands on boys. "[P]atriarchy demands of all males that they engage in acts of psychic self-mutilation, that they kill off the emotional parts of themselves." With these words, bell hooks strikes straight to the heart of the matter. If we truly "feel" our emotions, then we must "feel" each other and cannot dominate by force or other acts of cruelty.

When we generalize about men, of course, we're not talking about all men: gender cannot be separated from class when we analyze dominance, and, in America especially, gender also determinatively intertwines with race. To name white men as the locus of an unjust system is not to blame particular individuals. As with all theories about social systems, we are all entangled in them and, to one extent or another, complicit in their endurance: a perfect example of dialectical complexity or "both-and." Many individual white men demonstrate enormous compassion, gentleness, insight, and so on. If that were not true, we might simply be examining biology. But variations speak to the centrality of social factors. Some of those are cultural and interpersonal. From birth, boys are encouraged to suppress emotion: "Buck up, little man!" Adult men tend to play more physically with male babies, while girls may be more often coddled. Gendered toys of course become unavoidable. Even teething rings are colored pink or blue.

Beyond all these ingrained cultural habits, systems compound the training. Recent advances in promoting women's athletics are welcome, but the world of team sports is still dominated by maleness and sponsored by money. That boys learn to bond through doing, girls through talking may be a broad generalization, but like many such grand sweeps, it contains nuggets of important truth.

Laced through all these differences is the specter of violence. Even in times of peace, war lurks in boys' consciousness. Raising two male children, we banned weapons from our women-centered household—to little avail. The boys made sticks into guns, sneaked toy swords under their beds, read stories of battles and warriors. Neither of these children was violent; both avoided fights whenever possible. But both, one white, the other brown, were sometimes challenged, forced to make the decision whether to pacify or engage. Whether they wanted to or not, they had no choice but to negotiate violence.

Dynamics of masculine identity formation transcend color lines and, at the same time, impact people of different races very differently. In the stories that follow, I look specifically at how some individuals of color learn who they are, imbibing beliefs about what they can and cannot expect from life, how to stay safe, and where to find nurturance. I repeat: none of the injuries these boys and men sustain is the fault of individual white men, but all are inflicted in the house that white patriarchy built and continues, globally, to own.

Inscribing Racism in the Day-to-Day

Racism in America lives in many domains all at the same time. It is a historic legacy. It is hard baked into the economy. In other places globally, it may derive from colonialism or other forms of resource exploitation. But whatever the specific circumstances and histories, it universally imposes criteria for distributing social capital such as education and employment as well as other forms of material and emotional well-being. It secures rules of operation for organizations that construct inequality. It inhabits social interactions in daily life. It occupies mental and emotional spaces with individuals' minds and emotions. How do we teach children to accept beliefs about innate characteristics of races different from our own? First, by teaching them not to talk about the subject.

Not long ago, I encountered an interaction that illustrates how that happens. It also contrasts with Adi's story in a meaningful way. I liked to shop in a store a few blocks from my home in San Francisco. Family-owned, it was a friendly place, its products thoughtfully curated by health-conscious owners—a little overpriced to be sure, but worth it to me for its convenience and aesthetic pleasures. One day, as I pushed my cart around the aisles, I repeatedly crossed paths with a Black mother and boy I guessed to be about four, a rare sight in this upscale shop in a city where the African American population, driven out by gentrified housing prices, had declined in recent years from twelve to five percent. Somewhere around the many shelves of breakfast cereal products, I overheard a young white child exclaim to his mother, "Look, Mom! Why does that kid have funny hair?"

I froze, keen to witness the interaction and ready to do something—I wasn't sure what—should intervention seem warranted.

"Shhh," said the mother. "Don't be rude." And she hustled the child away to another aisle.

The Black mom looked steadily away from the whole encounter. "Which cereal do you want?" she asked her son in a voice that sounded to my ear painfully strained. I thought it was an understandable but unsuccessful attempt at distraction, and perhaps at consolation.

What lessons were taught that day to the two children? And what can we learn by contrasting this story with Adi's quest? First and most obviously, both children no doubt registered their mothers' distress, and these emotional lessons, we know, run deep. Most obviously, the encounter taught both children to be silent. "Don't speak" is an injunction we internalize early and in many forms. If words in general can be dangerous (Don't use that word! That's not polite! You'll hurt your grandmother's feelings), words connected with race are especially so. What feelings did the Black child intuit? Perhaps that his mother was angry, or frightened and protective of him. Looking around the environment and seeing how few other people there were present who resembled him and his mother made the connection with race obvious.

Meanwhile, the white child almost certainly registered his mother's alarm. To express aloud recognition of a difference between himself and the other child created a need to move away rather than toward the other. That impulse is the opposite of what I've been describing very young children experience. Lucy moved toward the mirror, Adi toward his adult friend Shelby. Rather than separating from Shelby, Adi empathically associated with her, relating his experience to hers. Why was Adi able to make that empathic reach? For one thing, because she was familiar, she lived in his world, ate at his table, knew and loved the people he knew and loved. That the white child used the word "funny" speaks of the contrast. Had he ever seen a child of African heritage before? Just how segregated was his world?

Institutional forces separated the two children even as their corporal selves interacted in the cereal aisle. Living in a city so largely segregated by housing costs (among other factors), the boys may well have felt an association based on age and gender, and perhaps the stresses of shopping with one's mother. But whatever identification they felt was cut off by their mothers' emotional reaction to the white child's curiosity. What might have been different if she had been able to say, "Yes, isn't it lovely? I haven't seen that boy and his mother shopping here before. Let's go over and say hello." Her welcoming response would suggest something positive, attracting attention rather than prohibiting it.

We can't know for sure why that particular woman went so automatically toward reproval rather than inclusion, but from my work on similar dynamics with many groups of people, I have seen numbers of comparable interactions. Often, white people say things like, "I was confused and worried it would seem racist if I approached the child and his mother." Or, "I didn't want to embarrass the other child and his mother." Or, "I was taught it is rude to speak to strangers; it's my responsibility to teach my child good manners."

In all these cases, the focus is on the discomforts, imaginings, and acculturated responsibilities of the white mother, not on facilitating friendly interaction. Had her son commented on some appearance of another white child, most of the restrictions might have been absent and the messages she inadvertently conveyed very different. Similar dynamics are very common in cross-racial social interaction among adults: the benefits of reaching out with friendship are overcome by fears, concerns, or rules of the white participant. Like Adi's intuition about Shelby's emotional state, every child imagines a story in order to make sense of their perceptions. When the adults around them express distress, tightness, withdrawal, two things happen: first, the child understands they must not question further; and second, they internalize the adult's fear, an emotion so compelling that it becomes closely associated with multiracial encounters.

Passing encounters like this one in the grocery store paint lines of separation in vivid colors. Both children, white and Black, experience not just difference but also values attached to this particular difference. Both children are taught not to question. The rule of silence is perhaps the most powerful socializing force imposed on young people. But this particular silence hangs heavily in another reality, this one social. One child is in, the other out, one "majority," the other "minority." In that upscale store, in a city where gentrification produces a severely imbalanced demographic, both children easily observe that one child looks like most people present, the other does not. And the one who is different is also identified to the white child as somehow a problem, a challenge, a source of discomfort and, maybe, danger. Even before the encounter in the store, something had cued the white child to describe hair different from his own as "funny." Why not "curly," or, simply, different? I see this story as a demonstration of the ways we form knowledge: the child's lived experience formulated in the context of unfamiliarity imposed by social structure and then given form and language by the interpersonal dynamic with his mother. All three realms twine together to enforce an identity and a powerful injunction: you are white; don't speak openly about racial difference.

Other forms of identity are also implanted early and hard. I've talked about gendered toys, but babies are gendered even earlier these days, in the womb. No longer is there that joyful surprise at the moment of delivery: "It's a girl!" Class may be less easily named but nonetheless deeply experienced. Domestic service, for one example, teaches the youngest of children about class, whether the youngster is served or recognizes that a parent or other adult close to them gives service. One young adult I know, the mixed-race child of a Latina mother and Black father, went to work with his housekeeper mother in a white family's home. At the age of five or six, they were told to "take care of" the younger white siblings. On reflection, when they told this story as a grown person, they realized they were probably told simply to play with them. But they deeply understood the complex unspoken instruction: their role was subservient, to give care not to receive it, and, most overtly, to raise no protest.

School, Prison, and Other Forms of Enforced Racism

I've mentioned a research project I conducted with people living in Little Rock at the time of the drama surrounding desegregation of Central High School in the 1950s. While I focused on oral histories of white alumnae from the year of turmoil, I also talked with many members of the African American community who had been affected. Again and again, people described the protections of their segregated communities back then, a phenomenon I witnessed still existing forty years later when I conducted my research. One major highway runs through the city. I stayed in a lovely bed-and-breakfast off the exit that led in the opposite direction to what was still a predominantly Black neighborhood. Coming back to my quarters at the end of the day, I noticed that every car exiting to the right contained occupants who were Black, while everyone exiting to the left was white. Men from the Black community again and again described to me their shock and confusion when they were eight or ten and first ventured beyond the dividing line. I heard so many stories of how they were met with hostility. Sometimes it was just suspicious glares from white shopkeepers and pedestrians—perhaps not so different from what the African American child in the grocery store picked up. Often in the Little Rock accounts, though, white teenagers shouted racial slurs, chased or otherwise harassed the younger Black kids. Such a huge contrast with the safety of a community in which adults tacitly agreed to look out for all children conveyed deep information about the nature of the world these boys would inhabit as men. Even at that young age, they began to strategize how to respond: with caution, challenge, invisibility, or withdrawal? Each line of possibility carried life-changing impact.

As I got to know people better and they described with more subtlety how they felt about desegregation four decades after it happened, many told me about losses that for them outweighed gains. Marian (a pseudonym), the mother of seven, described the problems in personal terms:

> I have two sets of children; it was about an eight year span between the two sets of children. So my first set grew up in a segregated school. But the last ones, they were in integrated schools.
>
> Well, my first set of children, they were taught by all Black teachers. And the teachers seemed concerned about the children, they worked with the children. . . . But once the schools integrated and the children started having white teachers, the white teachers did not relate to the Black children like the Black teachers did. Some of the children . . . did not do as well as my first set of children did. Because my first set of children really excelled in school, but these last ones who went did not do as well. They did fair, average, but not as well as they could have done.

Marian's evaluation of the impact of desegregation on her younger children speaks to the interplay between interpersonal, institutional, and cultural realities. Student bodies were integrated but not faculties. White teachers, steeped in the culture of southern racism, knowing nothing better and no doubt offered no instruction, denied Black children the attention and nurturing they gave white students. The children drew inevitable conclusions: when I visited Central High thirty years later accompanied by an older teacher,

Jerome, one of the still-minority Black faculty members, we walked down a corridor lined with classrooms that were thoroughly segregated. Jerome had told me that the school was now fifty-fifty, Black/white. Why were those statistics not reflected in the classrooms? I questioned.

"These that are mostly white kids are advanced placement classes." He pointed across the hall to one where Black teens sat in rows. "And those are regular classrooms."

I asked to visit the latter. The teacher, an older white woman, welcomed us. I asked if I could talk with her students, and she agreed with southern grace. I asked a few warm-up questions about what they were studying and how they liked the subject matter, getting embarrassed reticence rather than stirring replies. Then I took the plunge:

"I can see there are lots of white students at Central as well as Black. Why is it that so many classes are all white or all Black?"

They shrugged.

"I also noticed during lunch period that the tables on the west side of the building were filled with Black kids, the ones on the other side all white. Why is that?"

Silence. I let it lengthen. Finally, a boy toward the back of the room said, "It's just that the smart kids want to hang out with smart kids, and the rest of us hang out together."

How much pain is packed into that answer, how much oppression! That boy had internalized a view of himself and his friends that demeaned not only their intelligence but also their rights: to the best possible education, to respect for how they think, for whatever other rights? At the same time, there was a strong sense of identity with others who shared Black identity. In retrospect, I wish I had asked the white students why they hang out together. In other circumstances, white kids have described this social sorting by race in terms of the Black kids' choice, not theirs: "They separate themselves." A book by the psychologist Beverly Daniel Tatum called *Why Are All the Black Kids Sitting Together in the Cafeteria?* frames the question as a problem of the Black kids. Why did all the Jewish kids in Fort Worth socialize together? The directionality of the question reveals the answer: because we know we are the ones at risk, we are the ones separated out in so many different ways.

Confronting Violence: Interpersonal and Institutional

Remembering this conversation in Little Rock almost thirty years ago and knowing that academic tracking still separates kids in racially skewed ways, I wondered how teenagers might answer my question today. I consulted my friend and colleague Hasshan Batts. Hasshan heads a community organization in Allentown, PA. When violence threatens to explode on the streets, it's Hasshan people call on to intervene. His relationships with young members of the community give him a rare standing to interrupt moments of strife that might otherwise lead to injury or death.

"How would the youth you work with answer my question? Would they describe themselves as 'not smart'? What is the self-image they've internalized in today's world?"

"Troublemaker," Hasshan promptly replied. He went on to frame that remark in terms of a universal objective of teenagers (and the rest of us!): safety. Unlike the children in the segregated neighborhood in Little Rock seventy years ago, these contemporary Black kids find little or no assurance that they will be seen or protected by adults, whether known or strangers. So challenged has life become in communities of color like Hasshan's that adults, struggling to maintain their own survival and dignity, are largely absent from the places children grow up. Once out in risky public spaces, therefore, kids turn to peers for those protections, and for the boys in Hasshan's community that means gangs. So they become criminalized, even though often the packs kids form have no intention to engage in criminal activities. The more they are seen as criminal, however, the more they act to expectation. We all do that; sociologists describe the phenomenon as "labeling theory." Once labeled a doctor or a patient, a woman or a man, a parent or a grandparent, our own internalized assumptions about what the role entails set in, reinforced by reactions we get from people around us. "Doctor" gets you respect and a high income. "Criminal" makes you feared and lands you in prison. Nothing describes the sorry state of race relations in America better than statistics on incarceration, a dramatic consequence of injustice literally hidden behind bars:

- 37 percent of all people in prison as I write are Black, compared with 13 percent of people in America who are Black. The vast majority of them are male.

- Of people serving life sentences, almost half are Black.

- 30 percent of people on probation or parole are Black.[1]

Before our conversation ended, Hasshan added one more element to the discussion: "And they get pathologized." I'll be looking into this connection in Chapter 6; for now, the connection contrasts sharply with the experience of the boys in Central High School years earlier. To believe oneself to be inadequate, to lack mental acumen, leads to life choices that are closely aligned with class. You may take up a trade rather than go to college. Or you may drop out altogether, convinced that there's no point in trying to find a job. But unless you choose a life of crime, the attribute you've taken on is personal, not systemic. It interacts with and entraps you in severely painful and life-restricting racist assumptions which themselves form institutional boundaries. But it does not subject you to the overt methods of control facing Hasshan's youths: incarceration or psychiatric confinement. The diagnosis of oppositional defiant disorder, for example, on one level a description of interactions as seen from the perspective of the person being defied, on another level has life-altering consequences. One study of people in the United States admitted to inpatient psychiatric facilities over a six-year period showed proportions from white and Black people approximately reflecting the general population (lower for Latinos, Asians, or others). However, virtually all the Black admissions were court ordered, while all but a very few of the white ones were voluntary.[2]

Whether in prison or psychiatric institution, such physical containment creates lasting bars. Seen as dangerous, treated violently by authorities of the state, men of color, especially Black appearing men, daily face a very present risk that the fact of their physical attributes rather than their behavior will make them victims of violence, from the state or from other men. I remember my surprise when a client, a six-foot-something, physically able, distinguished-looking, middle-class Black man, told me he was always afraid when he walked down a street after dark in America. How striking that reversal was: in the cultural stereotype, *he* was to be feared. But in reality, he was the one most in danger. One of Dr. Hasshan Batts' most essential accomplishments has been supporting the mothers of murdered sons in his community. This destiny—jail, looney bin, or death—tracks men of color, especially those who are Black, throughout life.

If we fear that the people we oppress given an opportunity will oppress us, then we need to keep them securely under our heel. While the consequences are borne most acutely by people of color, white people too are impacted. Why are so many white Americans ending up tranquilizing themselves with drugs and alcohol? An undercurrent is this: if I am a white man, I have a choice to make: do I identify myself with the oppressor or do I too risk being oppressed? Later, I'll discuss dichotomies like this. If we're trained to think in opposites and binaries, then we're constantly confronted with Hobson's choices and the structure of patriarchy is secured.

How Color, Gender, and Class Set Limits to Ambition

Donald Trump vigorously exploited this dynamic to energize his rise to power. Joining demonization of immigrants with specters of criminal men of color and unfairly upwardly class mobile women of color, he established white people as the only legitimate, "legal" people entitled to have a voice in the United States. In the process, he demonstrated how much the binary of a Black-white population division obscures the reality of discrimination against people of other races. Brown Americans especially become hostage to daily jeopardy as the administration makes good on its pledge to expel "illegals." Yet many people categorized racially in this way have roots in this country far deeper than my own. A driver I encountered recently told me his ancestors arrived in New Mexico in the 1700s, almost two hundred years earlier than mine. Nonetheless, he stood on alert for possible confrontations with immigration officials looking for people to deport.

All Americans excepting a very few surviving indigenous people are descended from immigrants. A day without immigrants in America is a day without fruit harvested, hospitals cleaned, scientific research progressed, and so many more activities on which everyone, citizen or not, depends. My immigrant grandparents bequeathed me the genes that enable me to "pass" as white. That accords me unearned privileges, including the assumption that I am law abiding, even while I jaywalk, minimize my income on my tax return, and regularly break the speed limit. I grew up believing not only that I had a right to self-determination but also that I had the brains and the capacity to access it. For so many others, the experience of growing up in America is very different.

Eladio is a fitness instructor in the city where I live. In weekly exercise sessions at the small gym he owns, he has helped keep my aging body fit even as he's moved my heart with his inquiring mind and personal story. He illustrates one of the paradoxical consequences of the human capacity to extract strength from childhoods spent dodging violence and finding paths through deprivation. The reality of who he is defies the stereotypes, even while he himself internalized some of the lies about him. I see in his story a strong example of how small children make decisions about themselves that serve as both protection and limitation, as compliance and resistance all at the same time. It also speaks to our capacity to continue shaping and reshaping a sense of self as we experience more and more of life and integrate options to which we had no earlier access.

The first-born child of teen parents who moved away from their Texas families to a town in New Mexico, Eladio is descended from people who migrated from Mexico and earned citizenship two generations back. As we worked out, Eladio peppered me with perceptive questions about my work and beliefs. I was very soon impressed with the depth of his curiosity and eager to understand more about his roots and worldview. I delighted in our conversations, even while I labored at the exercises, and I praised him for his skill at both enterprises. At the same time, I picked up how profoundly he downplayed his intellectual acumen, even as he demonstrated it again and again. Over coffee one day, he told me more of his history, and especially how he came to define himself in terms of personal strengths and weaknesses.

Growing up, home was chaos. Isolated from elders and from a supportive community, enmeshed in all the stresses of the nuclear family, both parents worked dutifully all week and then drank heavily on the weekends. Fights, sometimes physical, were common. His father withdrew from family life except at those moments of drunken rage, and his mother regularly and harshly lashed out at the children. As younger siblings appeared year after year, Eladio sought whatever privacy—and sanctuary, I suspect—he could find.

School offered little refuge. His elementary school was shuttered a few years after he left for middle school because its students so regularly failed to meet even minimal state testing requirements. Heavily populated with Latino children, nothing he remembered spoke to anything in his lived experience. Classrooms, packed to capacity with unteachable numbers of students, were little more than holding spaces until children could be passed along to the next school. When that happened, Eladio found middle school little better than grade school. By then, however, he had made some clear decisions about himself: he was strong but not smart; he would make his way through sports, not grades. The first attribute was not surprising. Athletics had already become a centerpiece of his life, a place he excelled and was lauded. But I questioned why, like the teenager in Little Rock before him, he thought he was not smart. "Nobody ever said I was," he reflected. "Nobody ever paid attention to my thoughts or ideas."

But if no adult respected his brains, his peers were all too attentive to his brawn. Fighting among boys was common. "There started to be gangs in elementary school and lots of violence among kids. But I never joined." Why not? "I knew violence at home. I just decided I was not going to fight." Bullying among boys was a common thing. Eladio told a story of standing up for one of his friends and feeling pride that he could chase off the offender without himself being violent. While he rejected gang membership, he bonded with four friends. "We shared all the same values as the gangs: loyalty, protection, trust." I asked where the other four were now, and he froze slightly. "Three are either in jail or have been; the fourth is in the military."

Life changed when he started high school. For reasons Eladio didn't exactly understand, he found himself enrolled in a school on the "other side" of town: the white side. In his own neighborhood, everybody was poor. "We never went without essentials, but there was never anything much extra, either." In this new world, people lived in homes with excess space—"some of them even mansions, huge!" Before high school, he had understood differences between Latino and white people. But now suddenly class mattered. And right along with this new dimension of identity, Eladio felt a new emotion: shame. I questioned the link, and after reflecting briefly he said, "I'm not sure why, but I so strongly understood that being poor made me inferior."

"How did you handle that?" I asked, my heart heavy.

"I doubled down on being strong. And I knew I was appealing to the ladies, too," gesturing to his handsome face.

"Was there any teacher you liked? Anyone who recognized anything more about you?"

"There was one teacher in elementary school who liked my creative writing." We talked a bit about how that was, although I noticed some gestures of discomfort. Eladio soon pivoted to an account of success on the football team and other sports. I might have missed two words that told me he also excelled at academics. "I graduated high school *with honors* and chose to attend New Mexico State University. Even with a scholarship and my working, college was expensive."

So how did this "not smart" boy end up graduating with honors and being funded to a college education? Not football but academic excellence earned that financial help. In his junior year, he participated in a research project about neuroscience and Latino youths. When he graduated ("in five years, because I worked pretty much full time throughout"), he was recruited to a graduate program in neuroscience at an out-of-state, very prestigious university. Here, Eladio's narrative expressed evident pain.

"I didn't last long there. I ended up in the hospital and left after a few months. I wasn't cut out for it."

Shame fairly rolled off Eladio's demeanor as he told me this part of his story. I thought of all the brilliant people of color in my field who suffer intense shame because they could not complete doctoral programs. Coursework was doable, but writing a dissertation required them to think and write in a cultural mode so in contrast to their natural bent that they ultimately dropped out, carrying the scarlet letter of ABD (all but dissertation) forever seared on their dignity. I told Eladio how mad I felt about the injury to these colleagues and friends, how sad that such talent remained undermined in professional fields by lack of a credential, and how unjust I thought his self-blame to be. This culmination of the failure of the education system is one of many lying at the heart of continuing racial exclusion and class stratification.

A lawsuit in New Mexico, *Yazzi/Martinez v. State of New Mexico*, is currently in the courts, accusing the education system of ignoring the cultural needs of its predominantly Latino and Native American students, a fact made obvious by the state's standing near the bottom of educational testing comparisons. When a system insists on a singular cultural voice, and even more a highly restricted linear way of thinking and understanding the world that in no way conforms to the lived experience of so many of its students, then inequality is predetermined.

At the end of our coffee date, I asked Eladio if there were one word that, in his deepest self, describes him to himself. He replied promptly, "Gangster!" Surprised—not only had nothing in his story suggested anything other than an upstanding law-abiding citizen, but also because he was so clear that he had intentionally rejected the path of criminality and violence—I asked him to elaborate. Silent for a long, reflective beat, at length he said, "Outsider, refuses to join, my own person."

It is my practice to share with people who have so generously agreed to be interviewed for any of my projects what I write about them. When Eladio read my account of our conversation, he wrote back with this longer explanation of the "gangster" reference:

"My inner gangster is a member of my entourage that has helped me through adversity. It's an archetype characterized by grit, strength, and unwavering loyalty. This archetype among others, has helped me to succeed despite growing up in oppressive systems. Other archetypes might be the Athlete and the Thinker. Each of these members of my entourage has served me at various points in my life. As you illustrated, I have embraced that the Athlete and Gangster have helped me to be successful while overlooking contributions of the intelligent Thinker."

Now a successful small business owner, husband, and father, Eladio feels all the stresses and contradictions of the good life he's made for himself. Small business in America is a recipe for constant stress. As a fitness coach, Eladio is a star, and his personability carries him a fair distance through the challenge of promoting his business in a competitive market. But he struggles with the pendulum of pleasing his clients ("I'm a habitual people pleaser") and standing his ground when financial and training matters demand assertiveness.

Early in our friendship, when Eladio described to me the choice he'd made to play to his physical attributes and not his intellectual ones, I commented, "I see that as a way you've been impacted by racism."

He looked surprised and thoughtful. "Really? Nobody has ever said that to me before." That, I thought, defined one element of the oppression he has experienced and so steadfastly works to overcome: even when he comprehended the limitations to his life choices, he had been deprived of a word identifying those limitations as oppression imposed from without rather than deficits of his personhood.

Much has changed since the 1950s and even the 1990s when I did my study in Little Rock. Alas, Eladio's story suggests to me how much has stayed the same. What I heard from the teenager in Little Rock reflects many, many encounters that child had and many, many slights he'd observed and many, many racial slurs he'd heard or found in supposedly color-blind textbooks. All those experiences fitted him to take a subservient "place" in a racist culture. Eladio came to adulthood better prepared to find a competent place in society but still carries wounds of self-deprecation that threaten to limit his options. However effective his choices, many were eliminated: to be a neuroscientist, to accrue social and financial capital that relieved him from the daily strains of life, to hold himself as equally capable and entitled to whatever community supports are availed to his white peers.

Nobody (I hope!) overtly tells white kids to hold themselves superior to kids of color. When they are invited to enroll in advanced classes, with the clear implication that they will be rewarded with advantages when they apply to college—that they *will* apply and be accepted by a college—nobody tells them that they are being awarded racially privileged standing on the competitive ladder to success in a capitalist society. The high schoolers occupying those high-achieving physics and math classes may be focused on tests and grades and competitive standing among their peers. But beyond their awareness, they are also being fitted for their "place" in a white-privileged society, just as the Black and brown kids across the hall are being socialized to accept limitations to their possibilities.

Paradoxically, though, the white kids are likely to find their road toward security and happiness travels through some very rocky territory. Although on divergent courses in terms of choice and limitations, young people unknowingly embody a significant difference between the races: people of color tend to know they face socially imposed barriers; white people often do not. This contrast in perception of opportunity confuses people with relative privilege into believing they have freedom of choice, that they are masters of their fate. At the same time, they may experience a sort of moral pebble under the skin, a nagging sense of unfairness. Whether they know it or not, they are destined to collude with inequality bred into the patriarchy without reaping its richest harvests. But most often, that moral imposition becomes lost in the mist of normalization.

The white Little Rock alumnae, reflecting back on their role in the ending of legal school segregation, justified the inequity they knew to have been true. "It was just a way of life," they told me, a tint of guilt, a wave of defensiveness in their voices as they repeated the familiar phrase. Evoking nostalgic images of ideal circumstances, the ways these white southern women used the phrase blew a heavy smoke screen over all the injustices imposed by those ways. It was not coincidental that my interviews with white alumnae were almost all with women. At the very beginning of my project, a group of friends concluded that I was one of them: Texas-bred was a close enough affinity that they believed I'd understand their stories.

Patriarchy is a fundamental architecture to the social environment in which we live. How it affects women of all identities, racial and otherwise, is a key piece of the three-dimensional portrait I'm trying to draw in this book. For men, patriarchy creates a sharp distinction between those in the power elite and those not, holding out promise for white men that confuses recognition of the ways they are oppressed. For women, there is little promise of rising to the top of the power hierarchy. Instead, patriarchy sharply inscribes particular roles that come with particularly severe costs.

4 Generational Roles and Immigration
How Women Internalize Patriarchy

I was born in 1941. It was the year the United States entered the Second World War, the year of the Final Solution of the Jewish Question in Europe (i.e., the decision to exterminate all Jews worldwide), a year of deprivation as the Great Depression and the war economy intersected, and the year my sister turned two.

My parents were beyond stressed: two babies in diapers, born twenty-one months apart, while dad worked long hours and mom recovered from a back injury. I understood my operating instructions from the moment of my birth: "Beth is so independent!" everyone marveled. The repetitive observation translated to me as a command: "*Be* independent. Need nothing from us grown-ups!"

History both global and personal intersect to form us. Under these conditions, my father ignored me, and my mother handed me off to whoever she could. Fortunately, those people treated me very well. I believe the benign neglect I experienced did me a world of good. We make hay out of whatever grass we are handed.

For other girls in our family, though, the experience and the outcomes were very, very different. From a great enough distance, all detail disappears and we can see the grand sweep of the landscape. In that perspective, the terrain of patriarchy looks like this: males directed aggressively or protectively out toward the world, females forcibly turned inward to tend the home fires. For all the advances and variations on these broad themes, they do reflect a painful truth: men in general impose violence on others, while women all too often turn it on ourselves.

I include here a story I wrote for my family shortly after we had gathered for a cousin's funeral. It is a story, among many other things, of how women carry and enforce subjugation to systems of inequality on each other. As I listened to Eladio's story, to the power extracted, distorted, and embodied in his encounters with oppression, I thought about the similarities and, most painfully, the contrasts with my cousin Lynn's fate.

I went to my cousin Steve's funeral in Fort Worth, and I mourned my cousin Lynn.

Steve died a good death. At eighty-two, he reached the end of a decades-long containment of thyroid cancer. Getting the terminal diagnosis, he reacted with grace, humor, and practicality. A few weeks later, he died in his own bed, his son on one side, his daughter on the other, his best beloved poodle lying against his side, his second dog at his feet. The graveside ceremony his children organized was truly a celebration of life.

Lynn died by her own hand at the age of forty-two. If any ceremony marked her death, I had no knowledge of it. She married at seventeen, had a daughter less than a year later, and another a few years after that. By the time she was in her mid-twenties, she'd had a psychiatric breakdown and divorced. Lynn was brilliant and a beauty; recovering from both disruptive life events, she wrote a popular book about how to survive single motherhood, a status not too common in the 1960s, at least not for white, middle-class women. Unable to take her own advice, depressed and confused, she fled to the arms of lovers, one after another. All failed to produce the promised transformation of her life. When she committed suicide by overdosing on sleeping pills, she left no note. Her younger teenage daughter discovered her body, alone, soiled, contorted.

We were a set of seven cousins. In the first group of six, one born to each of the three siblings in my father's generation, Lynn was the eldest, Steve the youngest. Lynn, Judy, and my sister Nan were all born within nine months of each other. Twenty-one months later, I came along, with two Steves following in the next two years. My brother Rick straggled into the family five years later, fun to coddle, adored by my sister, but not of much interest to me. The Steves I held in disdain: boys and babies, yuck. As the eldest of the second set of kids, I was expected to play with them, and sometimes I did. But of course I yearned to be with my sister, with whom I was thoroughly merged, and my older girl cousins.

Lynn especially enchanted me. In our family, as in most, each of us acquired a fixed reputation almost at birth, repeated with prescriptive frequency throughout childhood. Lynn and I were the smart ones; she was also difficult, and I was also weird. I followed her with worshipful attention, even though she also scared me a little bit. She was fierce. Angry at her mother, cold to mine, she determined to go her own way, to escape I imagine, from the moment she could think. I was milder, at least until the teen years, but my most permanent reputation was, like hers, for independence.

Steve's life was not without trouble. After their divorce, his first wife mistreated and eventually abandoned their children. Steve embraced his role as a single parent, becoming the doting father hen. Once the children were grown, he married again—and again. Marriage was probably the only project that ended in something short of success. He established a career as a contractor, building gorgeous custom homes. The aesthetic sensibility that suited him for that work extended to art and to automobiles as well. When he died, two very costly cars lived in his garage, and the house he built for himself was filled with loved objects: antique tools, artworks he encountered at student exhibitions and from established artists, an eclectic range of things from many different cultures. Well-liked and respected by members of the tiny Jewish community as well as many of his clients, his funeral overflowed with family members and friends.

The sadness I felt at Steve's funeral was for his children's loss. I knew he left a large hole in their daily existence. The tears I wept at Steve's funeral were for Lynn.

A little before Lynn divorced, I left the country to live in India. So I missed some of the drama. But when I returned to the United States, a single mom with a three-year-old son, Lynn immediately embraced our commonality, wanting especially to extend advice about surviving as a woman on her own. She lived in New York; I soon settled in San Francisco. But we saw each other with surprising frequency for two years after my move back to the States, on my occasional visits east and hers west. In long, pained conversations, she opened herself to my sympathy and nurturing, something that ran counter to the family mythology about her coldness. I knew she was struggling with yet another relationship, this one with a psychologist who bedded her after she adopted him as her guru. Inevitably, that connection soon exploded, another disappointment in a long, long list of them. I knew she was suffering and when she asked to come visit, I agreed, setting the time after an impending work-related trip. The day I was to leave, she killed herself.

Our family represents many of the best things about families. My grandparents' and parents' generations took care of each other in multiple ways. Each parent pair was dedicated to giving their children the best chances in life they knew how to manifest. But Lynn's tragedy reflects another theme we embody, also like most other families: sexism. Two generations before us, my father's parents emigrated from Poland/Austria to New York, looking for relief from anti-Semitism and better economic chances. My father, the first-born son, became a doctor—a destiny, he often joked, he understood would be his as soon as he could understand what his mother was saying to him. Lynn's mother, Anne, was the sole daughter. The boys were given musical instruments to master because their mother believed they would never starve if they could play music. Morty, Steve's father, became a professional musician, playing in prestigious classical orchestras and in Broadway shows. My father worked his way through college and medical school playing trombone in speakeasies. Anne's musical genius remained unnoticed and undeveloped until it emerged in her own son and granddaughter.

Anne's destiny, equally clear from the moment of her birth, was to care for others, parents and brothers until she married, afterward a new family. That was a role she embraced with all the energetic brilliance submerged by her assignment; a role, I believe, she hated. Cooking became her creative expression; it took on a messianic urgency that aroused resistance and courted defeat. Daily she made meals for each individual in her family tailored to their idiosyncratic tastes. Instead of appreciation, she got complaints: too hot, too cold, too spicy, not spicy enough.

Lynn failed to bond. Recognizing from the start that this was a different sort of child, Anne overworked trying to please and, with increasing frequency, to pacify her. But nothing Anne did elicited affection from this strange child she was assigned to mother. Anne tried her best to satisfy what she believed to be Lynn's needs, contorting herself to produce whatever she imagined the child desired. The neglected younger sibling, the other Steve, retreated to his room. One day he cried, "All day it's Lynn this and Lynn that, but it's always dopey Steve!"

I breathed in all this troubled air and turned decisively away from Anne. Until I was ten and our family left New York for Texas, our two families lived half a block from each other, in a safe suburb near Manhattan. These were war years; all the adults lived with anxiety and distraction. Since my father's medical practice was housed in a wing of our home, my sister and I were often sent to Anne's house to play with our cousins. Anne, of course, wanted to feed us. I refused. I traveled back and forth clutching my own jar of Jiffy Peanut Butter. Anne tried to tempt me, producing this and that tasty dish—an exercise in predetermined failure. She relented and bought Jiffy Peanut Butter; I rejected hers, insisted on mine. I had speech difficulties, spoke a jumbled language nobody understood. Anne teased me, imitating my garbled communication failures. I gripped my peanut butter jar and set my jaw. Emulating Lynn, I fended off her mother with emotional ice. I bonded all the more securely with my cousin.

Fifty years have passed since Lynn killed herself. She crosses my mind from time to time but doesn't dwell there. So I was taken by surprise when news of Steve's death caused my throat to seize and my eyes to pour. A wise and earthy old friend once consoled me (was it for Lynn's death? I don't remember) with an image that has in fact consoled me through many deaths over the years. Each time someone dies, he said, the door between the worlds opens a crack, and all the loved ones he's lost peek through to say hello. He welcomes death, he said, for the chance to greet them all again.

But Lynn is more than peeking through that crack; she is screaming. Her cry is the anguish of a life stultified by restriction. She shouts of horizons drawn too close, of opportunities foreclosed, of stereotypes and assumptions that trapped her in the wrong life, in the wrong privileges, in the tragedy of miscasting that so painfully soon took her life.

I know now I'm mourning not just for Lynn the person but for Lynn the story. For her story is still too much the story of too many girls, too many women— too many others living so many different kinds of oppression and injustice. In this moment when our national leadership insists we are all equal in this land of unending opportunity, Lynn emerges from the other side to remind us—should we need reminding—that that is a lie, a lie so wrong, so unjust, so consequential that it injures us all.

My cousin Steve's children put together a lovely obituary for him. Listing the details of his life, they wrote him into vividness. Among other survivors, they listed all us cousins, but I noticed that Lynn was not there. That emptiness where her name should have been stabbed my heart with pain. My brother also noticed her absence, and he asked Steve's kids to correct the lapse. "Lynn," they replied, "who's that?"—and willingly added a phantom cousin to the list.

I hadn't planned to write this story. But all the way home from the funeral, my mind and heart filled again and again with a need to bring Lynn alive to this next generation who never knew her. Deprived once of that complicated, compelling kind of knowing, they deserve this other kind of knowing. And Lynn deserves it, too.

5 **Worldviews**
Individualism and Injustice

Each of us swims in waters we cannot see. So familiar, so essential to life is the stuff that we perceive its existence only with difficulty. Just as a fish's water is made up of hydrogen and peroxide, our conceptual medium similarly can be broken down into elements, including fundamental values, assumptions, aesthetics, tastes, beliefs, and orientations. There are various ways of naming this cognitive-emotional cloud in which all perception resides, all behavior flows, all relationships flourish or die. It is the standpoint from which we view the world, the worldview that situates us in a universe of people and ideas, or expectations and disappointments. It is the "way of life" we defend as it is challenged and look back on through shims of rosy, distorted memory.

While worldviews are three-dimensional constructs, they tend to be built on certain fundamental principles that define how we connect to the world in which we find ourselves. The nature of that connection is a beginning place from which to make visible the particular waters giving us life and keeping us confined to our own small pond.

Individualism or Collectivity?

The question "Who am I?" can never be separated from the larger question of my connection to others. We are both individuals endowed with certain qualities, tendencies, and more, and also products of a social matrix. Identity, then, embraces two aspects of who we are. Over many years, I asked students in my classes (and sometimes members of audiences at talks I gave), "What's your identity?" Members of oppressed groups invariably answered with the name of that social group: "I am African American/Jewish/gay/Latina . . . " White females often said "woman," but white men almost always named personal attributes: "I am athletic." "I am kind." "I am a procrastinator." (This last answer usually from students begging forgiveness for habitual lateness with assignments.)

That difference, between naming a group to which I belong and naming a quality of me as an individual, marks an important social fact. People who experience risk because of their social identity hold that identity in sharp definition. But those who have always occupied the center of the social matrix do not recognize an identity other than the personal.

One night when I was about five, as I lay in bed anxiously awake, I suddenly realized there were people in the world who hated me even though they did not know me. That was the moment I recognized viscerally my identity as a Jew. News of the Holocaust seeped through the walls of our home: newspaper images of survivors and, more powerfully still, in the embodied form of refugees who were briefly housed by my family. I knew something terrible had been done to them and, by my association through Judaism, could be done to me. Before that moment, being Jewish was for me a fact of absolute normalcy, indeed of comfort, barely registered. When the refugee woman who lived in our basement hugged me to her chest, I knew she sought my solace but also hoped to protect me. To my knowledge, everybody in my immediate world was Jewish. That moment when I recognized hatred in such a personal way led me to know with a new certainty that a boundary existed: who was inside, who outside? My identity as Jewish became cemented, and something beyond identity happened as well: I internalized the *meaning* of being Jewish. I was the other, different, potentially even hunted.

Worldview is a broad and elastic concept. It includes deeply held maps of the social world as well as rules of the road, the moral code we are taught and believe. Right along with learning who we are, we develop embedded assumptions about rights and risks, about agency and powerlessness, about privilege and exclusion.

"Jewish" was, of course, not the only category structuring my psyche. My sister and I were "the girls." We were gendered from the moment of our births. Our world mirrored that primary fact in every possible way. Most of those ways mapped out a plan for our lives. My father worked somewhere out there in the world. Even his home clinic was separated from the rest of our family life by bolted and curtained double doors. We knew that my mother's mandate was caring for everything domestic. World/male; home/female. My sister became the perfect manifestation of womanly capabilities. She loved to cook, doted on the new baby when our brother was born, feared strangers, and passionately preferred home to school. Twenty-one months younger, I took the opposite path. I longed to start kindergarten when my sister went, even though I was too young; imagined how I would support the family if something bad happened to my father; refused to set foot in the kitchen. Somehow, layered on top of my rebellion, I also understood that out in the world we would someday enter as adults, both my sister and I would *need* to have careers in a way our mother did not. We were securely gendered female, but the nature of femaleness was changing. Our essential cultural selves were engraved "Jewish" even as the world reckoned with a Holocaust that shook the meaning of that identity to the core. We did not yet know that once we were launched into the world as adults, people we met would identify us unquestioningly as "white," according to us privileges that only would become clear to us if we made an effort. We were "nanandbeth"/"the girls," female, white, Jewish—and I was Beth and my sister Nan, separate and distinct, all in the same moment.

Throughout history, this duality of identity has no doubt existed. We are both members of groups and we are separate persons. But in the capitalist era, a significant change took place that altered the relationship between those two aspects of identity. Where earlier, group had been the grounding sense of place, now that ground shifted to the individual side of the equation.

Capitalism transformed the nature of family and community. When western industrialization became the prevailing mode for producing goods, people's daily lives, attuned to the hours and needs of tilling land or creating crafts, shifted to the demanding clock of the factory. While a large share of the economic benefits of labor now as well as then are appropriated by a small number of people high in the social hierarchy, the means by which these class dynamics play out changed significantly. Large-scale manufacturing led steadily to the accumulation of populations in cities, a labor force disconnected from land or elder kin. Multi-generational families of yore severed into nuclear ones, two parents (and all too often only one) raising children and working outside the home for wages. Economic structures translate into character structures. The character needed to fuel these new industrialized forms was an unencumbered person, free to follow the job market, someone who considered himself (I've intentionally used a gendered word here) the master of his own fate. That is the concept called "individualism."

But humans are in essence social creatures. Babies cannot survive without human care; no more can adults thrive without companionship and love. Today's economic organization works against such durable social relations. Individuals experience alienation from more than the production process;

hardships of isolation and lonely responsibility for our own well-being, combined with the uncertainties of access to economic resources, fray the comforts of security and create emotional distress, especially loneliness and fear. This cognitive dissonance, the distance between "master of my fate" and "one paycheck away from homelessness" manifests as competitive behavior as well as emotions of shame and anxiety. "I should be able to succeed (as measured by my bank account) but my checkbook shouts that I am not succeeding. I am ashamed of my failure and don't want anyone to know. So I hold my own counsel and don't confess to anyone how frightened I am." Silence begets isolation, so we don't learn that our neighbor harbors surprisingly similar feelings, our affluent sibling too, and even the person we envy as the shining example of professional and personal success. The definition of "successful" seems fixed and finite when in reality it changes with the culture, the times, the economy, the technology, one's position and status in the social hierarchy, and possibly even the weather.

Capitalism tends to divide all sorts of processes into compartmentalized categories, a sort of reflection of the assembly line manufacturing process projected onto human affairs. To be alone, responsible, and powerless is a recipe for intense emotional distress. In this outsourced and monetized culture, solace for personal suffering is professionalized like so much else, placed in the hands of trained workers in a psychiatric industry that includes psychotherapists, counselors, psychologists, and a variety of other forms of mental health workers. The three pillars of modern life as lived in industrialized western societies are capitalism, psychiatry (both as it is practiced and as it embodies an ideology), and individualism. How do an economic system (capitalism), a medical profession (that carries heavy ideological consequence), and a cultural underpinning of national identity come together to both create what we know as the benefits of normal life and also lock us into serious issues of inequality, personal unhappiness, and isolation? I'll share with you a very personal story about stepping through a looking glass and finding myself in a very different reality frames, an experience central to the deepening of my worldview.

Swimming in a Different Pond

At twenty, fresh out of college, living in Manhattan and challenged by my first job, I fell in love with a self-exiled freedom fighter from India named Probhat

Roy. Soon we journeyed from the United States to join his extended family in a rural area some three hundred miles north of Calcutta (now renamed Kolkata). The rice-growing, riverine, mango tree-dotted landscape in which I found myself blew away webs of assumptions and beliefs. The lush vistas, everywhere entwined with dense tropical growth, mirrored a social landscape every bit as complex, fecund, and, to me, welcoming. People greeted me in surprising ways. Many of the villagers where my new family lived had never seen a white-skinned human before. They encountered me with as much wonderment as I them. The questions they asked me I found perplexing and soon reorienting. At first, I tensed for the kind of testing that accompanies new acquaintance in my western experience: people ask what you do, where you went to college, who made your clothing. Now, the questions I was asked were quite different:

Who are your people?
Where are they?
Where is that?
How do they feel about your being so far away?

It took little time for me to feel my body change. I relaxed, somatically registering the absence of something I had never been without before: nobody was judging me personally, no one assessing my looks or smarts or achievements against theirs. Nobody cared where I went to college or how much money my father made as manifested in my wardrobe. In this strange interpersonal landscape where competitiveness disappeared, my sense of self shifted and thinned. Instead, my awareness became centered on my social reality as people tried to place me in a network of relationships, assessing my standing in that web emotionally, not according to status.

Instead of individualism, the scrim always before clouding my vision, I was seeing people—and myself—through a prism of collectivity and relationship.

I soon learned that extended families and involuntary membership even in the most loving collectives may not always be a beloved experience. My young sisters-in-law had some critical things to say about it—as did the youngest brother of the extended family. Times were changing—as evidenced by my husband's sojourn half a world away. India was industrializing, and extended families were dividing. By the time I left India almost a decade later, we were living in an isolated apartment in a big city, raising an only child who knew his relatives as strangers appearing on rare visits and disappearing soon afterward.

Having replicated the unwelcome conditions I had known since my birth, and with the marriage breaking under the weight of isolation and my companion's disappointment in the post-independence political state of India, I reluctantly returned to America. But I could no longer see myself, or others, as detached from the social conditions shaping us. My "self" had morphed from distinct to blended. Broadly speaking, the contrast I felt in my tissues was between a collectivist self and an individualist one—between "I am because we are," and "I think, therefore I am."

This distinction is often difficult for people to grasp. Just as gender assignment is so repetitively engraved on our sense of self from birth, so too is this orientation to community. As with gender, we're talking here about something that is in reality fluid and dynamic, not a spectrum, not distinct categories. Where we fall on the spectrum at a moment in time, however, varies with important effect. The balance between individualism and the good of society is a question parsed in American legal discourse since the end of slavery. The Fourteenth Amendment, created in 1868 out of struggle for reconstruction after the end of the Civil War, established full citizenship for emancipated people. It also enshrined a right to privacy, elaborated in 1890 early in his legal career by (later) Justice Louis Brandeis in a *Harvard Law Review* article. "(T)he protection of society must come mainly through a recognition of the rights of the individual. Each man [*sic*] is responsible for his own acts and omissions only." (*Harvard Law Review*, Vol IV, December 15, 1890, No. 5) Brandeis (and his law partner Samuel Warren) begin their paper recounting how understandings of the right to privacy grew from addressing protection in a physical sense to something more spiritual: "the right to enjoy life,—the right to be let alone."

There is something to be said for this notion; it is the liberal principle that formed the basis for many of the most progressive legal rulings by the Supreme Court of the Twentieth Century. On its basis rests *Brown v. Board of Education*, which ordered the racial integration of public schools; a series of rulings protecting access to contraception, gay sex between consenting adults, same-sex marriage, and eventually the right to abortion (until it was repealed by a conservative court in 2023). One justice, John Harlan, contended that identifying the proper balance "built upon postulates of respect for the liberty of the individual . . . and the demands of organized society" was precisely the role of the Supreme Court.

Beyond the judiciary, what proves a functional resting point in that tension, I believe, is the well-being of a population. For white, urbanized occupants of the American middle class, the equation tilts uncomfortably toward the "it's all up to me, I'm responsible for my own fate, indeed for my own reality" side. Why does that matter? Among other reasons, if I stand alone in a competitive social structure, and if the resources needed for well-being are in scarcity—or, more accurately, unequally distributed such that the portion available to me and to others of my station is actually limited—then I must compete for whatever it is I need. To do that successfully, my capacity to compete must be at least roughly equivalent to that of my opponents. Fair competition assumes equality. But if I'm female, disabled, a person of color, an immigrant, and so on, that assumption is wrong. I'll go into this aspect of the problem in a later chapter. Here, I want to explore how the combined mythologies of meritocracy and individualism disadvantage everyone.

Distributing Rights, Obligations, and Expectations: The Plight of the Nuclear Family

Who I am bleeds into what I can expect, what I'm entitled to, and how I'm supposed to behave. Because families are more or less isolated units, depending on where they are and how they are located in the social order. A Black family living in a predominantly African American community, SY's family connected in very detailed ways with neighbors and relatives. She herself, however, was separated from this familiar grounding when she was sent away to "desegregate" white schools. My own family had slim connections with close relatives in New York but soon moved away to Texas where we belonged to a tiny Jewish community but lived primarily as an isolated nuclear group. Because this typical family structure is a primary breeding ground for racism, I start with a discussion of domesticity as it most typically is experienced by white, middle-class, urban people: the nuclear family, what sociologists call a "normative" family, that primary funnel for saturating young spirits with the cloud of capitalist misrepresentations. "Normative" is another name for "dominant." We all experience many different forms of culture, but not all forms dominate. My friend and colleague Mary Trujillo defines culture as "making meaning." Ways of doing that vary from one segment of a population to another, based on where and how people live. But everyone is subject to a set of assumptions and beliefs that must be adopted or contested. These ideas define "normalcy," even while they deviate from the lived experience of everyone in some ways and of some in many essential ways. While not everyone has membership in the dominant culture, I suggest that everyone is oppressed by it. Those whose identities coincide with the dominant majority, and therefore lie obscured by it, suffer harms very different from those who are marginalized by dint of their "othering." Karl Marx remarked that it is the ideas of the ruling class that become the ruling ideas. That's what I want to demonstrate by looking at this normative white, heterosexual family. Which also happens to be the sort of family in which I was raised.

Capitalism, as I've said, disconnects people in multiple ways. It lures people away from the places they've grown up and locates them in families isolated from earlier generations and severed from communities of support. I've said "lured," but my personal story illustrates a second force at work: raised in a nuclear family, I couldn't wait to get away. My own family had a stay-at-home mother and enough wealth to hire lots of help for her in running the household. Nonetheless, the disquiets of the adult lives around me suggested paths forward I in no way wanted to travel. My reaction may have been early and extreme, but the subsequent history of divided families, of adolescents who strike out to build lives far from home, of young people either turning away from parenting or determined to create alternative methods by not doing what their own families did: "I'll do the opposite of what my parents did to me!" all suggest that my own distaste for family as I knew it was not unique.

In my youth, middle class heteronormative white families tended heavily toward the gendered divisions of labor my family illustrated: mom at home, dad earning the money. What often resulted was an underutilized, lonely, and therefore disgruntled woman bound to the vacuum cleaner and the kitchen. Resentful of her husband's absence, and perhaps envious of his ability to engage a bigger world, she dedicated her genius to the raising of her children. This interdependence—she needed the outcome of her project to meet her expectations—or rather, the expectations placed on her—while the kids, having turned toward her for all their nurturing, resented her laser focus on them, experiencing it as control.

Meanwhile, men grew increasingly detached from emotional engagement with their children and also with their wives. In the early days of my work as a mediator, I did lots and lots of mediations with these kinds of couples. In each session, I took notes on the grievances people expressed. One year, I charted the complaints men and women made about each other. Hers focused on his inability to engage her intimately except in sex, his demands for which turned her off. His sketchily described how he disengaged from her because she nagged him constantly to "help" with the emotional and manual labor of the family. He also vented about her refusal of his sexual overtures. Most couples weren't yet even at the point of trying to share housework. That came later when the cost of living rose to impossible heights and middle-class women in these families lost the problematic privilege of full-time domesticity and entered the workforce. Then the "second shift" phenomenon became central to the conflicts I mediated: both parents in the workforce, only one doing housework and child rearing while the other "helped" reluctantly on demand. Arlie Hochschild, a sociologist, recorded this pattern, sitting in homes and noting who did what in fifteen-minute intervals. She published her results in a brilliant book called *The Second Shift*.

Socioeconomic contexts and histories call forth psycho-cultural dynamics that shape individuals beyond the conscious recognition of the people so shaped. If women do the majority of nurturing children, children turn toward them for nurturing, not fathers. Without the demand to nurture, and perhaps with feelings hurt by the child's preference for mom, men turn away from sharing the child-rearing labor. Meanwhile, both parents are stretched way too thin by too many hours of work, long commutes, and the second shift before and afterward at home. Because women typically earn less for an hour of work, the couple may decide she should cut back on hours while he, compensated more amply, takes on more. So he's even less available than his wife both to share the workload and also to build the relationships. Meanwhile, in her isolation at home, with no time to sustain friendships, she turns to him as her major source of companionship and support. He gives her advice; she seeks understanding. He needs rest; she needs help. He avoids conflict; she is desperate to talk it through; conflict is at least a point of connection. She grows increasingly insecure, knowing she is financially dependent on him. He feels increasingly burdened, locked into an alienated job with little creativity or fulfillment, but knowing the whole responsibility of supporting the family falls to him. These strains on the couple eventually break the marriage. In 2024 in the United States, one divorce was recorded every thirty seconds, almost a million in the course of the year.[1] Paradoxically, I sometimes witness fathers building deeper, more loving, more verbal relationships with their children *after* a divorce, when they find themselves in sole responsibility some of the time.

Benefit though that may be for men, for women the economic consequences are staggering. One third of custodial parents (a very few of whom are men) do not receive any child support. In the 1980s, the "feminization of poverty" was a buzz among sociologists and leftists. The gender earnings ratio improved some between 1980 and 2008, from a bit over 60 percent to close to 80, but it stalled there, still way under parity.[2] Tracing these dynamics so clearly illuminates the close interweaving of socially engineered gendered skills and proclivities with discriminatory structural dynamics. This same analytic lens reveals harm, similar in kind though perhaps different in detail, to people experiencing inequality in all forms: race, sexuality, disability, and so on. Without fundamental changes to social relations, not only does the oppression roll on, but it also remains invisible to those who are advantaged—even while they themselves suffer, too. Along with the harm to women in this case, men also are clearly wounded. They lose marriages on which they depend for their own human support and nurturing, and they may miss out on the richest rewards of parenting: children's love.

Through all this drama, what's happening to the children? They, too, are being shaped by the conditions they encounter. As Adi and Lucy demonstrate, youngsters figure things out early and often. Before a certain age, all they have to go on is their lived experience and what they understand of what people around them tell them. Adi lived in a peopled world: parents, sister, grandparents, friends, neighbors. Shelby, an important person in that constellation, was not to his knowledge living with anyone else he knew. So he asked the question: "Do you live alone?" I imagine even to formulate the question that way reflected substantial cognitive maturity. He might have extended his own experience and asked, "Who do you live with?" That he queried the opposite possibility—living alone—reflects a significant concept of difference.

So children figure out what is, what isn't, and what might be starting early and continuing into adulthood. Most of all, children formulate clear ideas of what pleases them and what doesn't. Adi knew he would be lonely without his parents and sister. On the other hand, children know very clearly what they don't want: peas on their dinner plate, going to bed when parents want them to, shampoo on their heads, being made to smile at an old uncle who smells bad to them. But knowing what you want doesn't mean you'll get it. Childhood in nuclear families is filled with normalized coercion. Parents' lives are structured by the industrial clock: get up in time for work and, eventually, school, which means meals at a certain time, a set bedtime, time for play squeezed in when other demands don't dominate. Time oppression is the rule, freedom the exception. Much of that clock is set by adult needs, not children's. Soon, awareness of what we want dims; if you can't achieve something, how painful it is to want it. I remember a moment when I stopped myself from wishing for some particular birthday present. These were war years, and I knew that so many things were in short supply. "If I wish for it," I told myself, "I for sure won't get it." That was a moment when I tacitly, sadly, consented to my own deprivation. Not getting had become the norm.

Submitting to Consent

"Normalization" means ideas that surround us with such uniformity that they are accepted without question by others and are so rarely questioned or contested that we come to assume they are facts of life, not human constructs with histories. In that amnesia, we cease to imagine what might be. We give in to the conditions we confront and have been told, in so many ways, are inevitable. The consensus about what must be accepted is not accidental. It lives in history and in the particular social system, forming a dominant culture that fits us for our roles in society. Because there is such a wide agreement about what's normal and what's possible, the dominant culture becomes hegemonic, dimming an ability to conceive of alternatives, rendered invisible.

The concept of cultural hegemony is a way of understanding how culture protects the privileges of elites by mystifying rights and entitlement and by ruling out of consideration the relevant social truths. Articulated in the 1930s by the Italian revolutionary Antonio Gramsci, the theory stimulated a workers' movement to create a counterculture. Vibrant centers were built where ordinary people gathered to create art, write alternative versions of their reality in their own authentic voices, make music, and more.[3] The spirit of resistance to the fascist regime of Mussolini then in power led to revolutionary actions, which, in short order, were quashed by the government. Gramsci himself died in prison; most of his important writings were smuggled out by friends and family, scribbled on whatever scraps of paper he could access. Especially relevant for our times, his objective was not only to build an autonomous culture for the working class, which he hoped would someday take revolutionary action to transform the country and the world, but also to enable an expansive coalition with rural folks who, in that day, formed a majority of the Italian population. The ideas he inspired in that very different context suggest pathways for our time and place, given a parallel need to transcend divisions that keep us all locked in place. To escape the hegemony of dominant ideas opens up possibilities for true multicultural collaboration in equitable and mutually respectful relationships. These ways of being, so difficult to imagine and to achieve within a narrower framework, emerge in the interplay of different peoples. In contemporary America, isolation compounds dominant culture to leave us ill-equipped to think in terms of complexity. We lose sight of the context for what we experience, and we forget that it wasn't always this way, that not everyone shares our culture, and that it might be possible for life to be organized radically differently. Rarely are we encouraged to think beyond what is, to imagine what might be. Imagination is stifled by isolation, reinforced by oppression.

I am suggesting that both parents' and children's lives are framed by oppressive conditions that allow little room for negotiation and change. If the adults must work on an unalterable schedule, then children have no flexibility in when they wake up, when and how they dress, when and what they eat for breakfast. If parents arrive at evening family time with exhaustion and the tensions of handling difficult encounters with other adults all day, then the children face caregivers whose capacity for care has been depleted before acts of caregiving even begin. No wonder parents look away from conflicts among siblings. No wonder the dinner table becomes a battle of wills: eat your peas; no I won't! No wonder bedtime turns from a sweet and quiet time reading stories to sleepy children to the quiet impatience of grownups and the restless insomnia of kids. No doubt I am overdrawing this picture. I know that many families manage to extract love and sweetness from all these pressures. But even that recognition contains a contradiction: "extract" suggests something not freely given, something stolen from a system designed to exploit the best of human interaction, not to enable it where it is most humanly rewarding.

My touchstone for "what might be" is the Bengali village where I lived in the late 1960s. Life in India was tough in those days. Drought and the aftermath of 1947, the year independence from British rule was declared, left severe food shortages. In the cities, rice was rationed. The village had no road and no electricity. Access was over a rutted dirt path, mostly by bullock, or horse-drawn cart. We possessed a rare automobile—how we'd come by it is another story for another time. The one and only occasion we tried to drive to Bajitpur, a crew of dusty, loin-clothed men led the way throwing dirt and cow patties into pits and over puddles, pulling and pushing us along. Our family compound was, like all the other structures in the village, built of clay and straw, although it was a bit grander than most homes: two stories and with a treasured well in the half of it occupied by my husband's uncle. Water was drawn by bucket and rope. Inside our half lived my mother-in-law, three brothers-in-law, two of them married, each with children, and an old beloved man, a teacher who had tutored the children of the family in their youth and thereafter schooled all the children of the village. Everything about daily life was collective. All the children were tended to by all the adults. In a highly ritualized separation of the genders, all the women cooked two major meals a day; all the men tended to the work outside the compound. Not that the women lacked voice; my mother-in-law set an example for informed opinion, frequently expressed and fully respected by the men.

It was the lives of the children that most pierced all my assumptions. For one thing, there was no conflict. My sister and I fought with each other constantly. Close in age, cast together most of the time, we were "the girls," our identity bounded by that nomenclature even while we were compared to each other very frequently. Nan was sweet and vulnerable, a perfect little homebody. I was independent and smart, impatient for the moment I could leave home. These reputations were grounded in something real at the same time that they were seriously flawed. I longed for nurturing and recognition, Nan for … I'm not sure what: perhaps confidence and a sense of safety. We took our deprivations out on each other, teasing and goading and quarreling about everything.

In Bajitpur, the children were a cohesive pack. Kids of all ages played together, exploring the land beyond the compound and inventing games inside it. Among themselves, toys and games were easily shared in multi-age groupings, with no competition or possessiveness. While we had been free to play outdoors, mealtimes were set by my father's working schedule. Here, children were fed by mothers at whatever moments they felt hungry and asked for food. There was a rhythm to mealtimes but only a loose one and never enforced. Big pots of curries, rice, and lentils bubbled in the kitchen all the time, tended by all the women collectively. Contrast the ease of this approach with classic dinner-time strife in a western nuclear household. Insisting children eat when adult schedules demand institutes alienation from the body as well as from the small society. Kids rebel in many creative ways, all involving overt or covert conflict. Meanwhile, one parent in the kitchen, usually female, understandably wants everyone fed and finished at the same time. The more peaceable Bajitpur system is made possible by the sharing of labor among many women. Children remain free to experience their own bodily needs. The only time I saw any friction between children and parents was around bathing, the one strict ritual of the day and the one rare time some kids protested.

We all imbibe ideology with our daily bread—or *chapati*. In the village, the children of our family knew they occupied a place of privilege in a class structure. They were Brahmin; their family-owned land farmed by tenants. Their fathers laid no hand on till or bullock; they dealt in more abstract matters of money and polity. While the family children had close relationships with village children, and while they all went home at night to homes built of clay and straw, there were distinct markers of class and caste. Children internalized knowledge of their social place; they experienced that location in collective terms: *we* are Brahmin; *we* are destined to be educated; and so on. Their individual identities held far less force than their shared ones.

The absence of conflict among the children was most striking to me. As I got to know more and more families, saw dynamics in Bajitpur and other villages, talked with parents and other adult caregivers, and most of all as I noted differences between the conditions under which children grew to adulthood in the United States compared with rural India, I was inspired to imagine how the circumstances of one translated into the other reality.

The first and most obvious contrast speaks to the impact on all of us, little and big, of scarcity. The isolation of American children stands in vivid contrast to the multi-aged packs of children playing and living together in Bajitpur. Sibling conflict is often interpreted to be competition for parental attention or love. That may be a strand in the dynamic, but I think also of vivid comments I've heard made both by children and by adults about childhood. In our seventies, my sister and I mused about our relationship as children. We were driving somewhere with our mother, then in her early nineties. "Why did we fight so much?" I mused, thinking it a rhetorical question. To my surprise, my sister immediately responded with intensity: "Because *you* were always there!" So many years later, the emphasis in her voice spoke of the impact of the experience many decades before.

Why did it matter to her that I was always there? No doubt I could be pesky. Even though her experience of life without me had only been twenty-one months, nonetheless she knew that absence as a possibility. I did not. For her, my birth was a change. For me, my sister's presence was the only reality I knew. She represented constant companionship to me, while I was a dramatic alteration of her peopled landscape. For both of us, adults were in scarcity. War compelled their attention in many ways. Our father was gone long, long hours, working for the military as well as providing for medical needs in the community, substituting for doctors serving abroad. My mother contended with many kinds of scarcities: of materials and foods and the availability of labor. We lived in a suburban neighborhood where it was reasonably safe for us to roam and explore, once we were old enough for that. But there were few children: we were born just as war induced a dip in birth rates. So we were cast together just as my sister said, "Always!" We shared a room; when we played with cousins or the siblings across the street, we played together. There was no television yet; the internet was not even a distant fantasy. So we had to make play up as we went along, an arena of clashing desires and creativity. I wanted to make things; she wanted to role-play.

In today's world, this isolation of siblings in nuclear families is compounded by danger in public spaces. Today's kids are confined within walls for much of the time. Class and race associate heavily with the degree of risk to children beyond their homes. Inner city children living in neighborhoods where violence is a common fact of life are, of course, at greater risk. But risk is also a subjective phenomenon. How worried are parents? When my son was a pre-teen, he reveled in learning the bus routes in the city where we lived. He could go anywhere. I was not exactly comfortable with his roaming; the sensation of distance between us, of my incapacity to protect him should he need protection, was something I worked at handling for the sake of nurturing his spirit of adventure and his growing skills in navigating the world. But then the first of a series of child kidnappings happened—right up the street from where we lived. Daily decisions—to let him play in the park, travel by public bus, go to the store by himself—became exercises in managing terror. A wise friend, an older man practiced in the ways of men and cities, convinced me that children were safer if they learned street smarts than if they were kept protected at home. And so we talked about scenarios, possible dangers, how to keep antennae alert for challenges and so on. These choices became more and more difficult as risks, or perhaps the perception of risks, grew over time. In the next chapter, I'll return to these themes in the context of class and racial differences, for they play out very differently depending on the realities of identity and place.

When my grandchildren were little, Mia, older by three years, sometimes grew angry at her younger brother's insistence on playing with her. Echoing ethics of earlier generations, she protested, "I need space!" She also sometimes called him names. We, supposed-to-be experts in human affairs, counseled her to tell him she was angry rather than trashing him. "But it feels so much better to call him names!" she countered.

Adults know that, too. In a conflict, raised voices, injurious judgments, and threats give us a sense of honest expression. We may know even while we scream that what we really want is to solve whatever problem is giving rise to the conflict. On some level, we know we're making matters worse, not better. But in the moment, we don't care; we scream invectives anyway. It feels so much better.

Letting off steam is a direct response to tensions built up while absorbing the costs of oppression. Parents do not mean to oppress their children: on the contrary. But on their own level, in their own lives, parents are also absorbing harms caused by all the actions and deprivations they are required to endure. When a breach occurs, steam releases. Where do kids direct that energy? Sometimes in direct conflict with parents. But even more often, in ways small and large, toward each other. Mariah Breeding's brilliant work on abuse between siblings demonstrates the extent to which siblings experience more violence inside the family walls than outside. Her work notes not only the phenomenon but also the ways in which it is normalized. As my sister and I reflected on the strife between us when we were kids, our mother, sitting quietly in the front seat of the car, interjected: "You girls never fought. You had a good relationship." We looked at each other in horror, both remembering how often our mother had said, "I only hope you grow up to have children who drive you as nuts with their constant fighting as you're driving me!"

Viewing the World All Alone

What do all these dynamics have to do with our theme in this chapter: individualism? How did I, some eighty years ago, understand that I would need to choose a career? How did Adi come to know that loneliness was a possibility? I've named three domains in which we construct knowledge of the world—and of ourselves in the world: lived experience, interaction with known others, and learning from many forms of media. From each of these arenas, children derive lessons in the relationship of self to others.

Individualism as an ideology suggests that I am a free agent, able to act on my own wishes and needs, and also responsible for my own successes and failures. For young children, there are multiple contradictions between this implicit instruction and the reality they face. Bounded by walls not always physical, by parental fears of danger beyond the home, by time constraints, and increasingly in the twenty-first century by the lure of electronics indoors, young children spend huge amounts of time at home. As the typical family size recedes toward two and a half, that time rarely allows kids to engage with other children. When they do, what's available to them may be only one.[4] Isolation from peers is therefore what most children experience, depriving them of ways to learn how to work out relationships without adult supervision.

Whether in childcare because parents work, or a little later in elementary school, kids do encounter others their age. But in these settings, most of the day is regimented. Time is structured by lesson plans; recess ends way too soon. Before long, kids recognize that they are being categorized and judged, compared against each other. Whether by subtle signals or more overt ones, children are taught to compete. Eager to participate, a bunch of students wave hands in response to the teacher's question: who gets called on? Kids notice and draw conclusions. Ample research shows that teachers recognize boys more frequently than girls. (see *Still Failing at Fairness* by David Sadker and Karen Zittleman, for example) Race also is determinative, white teachers calling on white kids disproportionately. By 2018, only 47 percent of public-school students but 79 percent of teachers were white.[5] However "woke" teachers may be, they carry the same cultural biases as the rest of the population. Racially associated cultural differences mislead adults grounded in culture-bound assumptions to overlook expressions of brilliance and talent in unfamiliar kids. Compound that dynamic with the pressures of teaching in public schools: class sizes too large, pay too small, hours too long. Where do overworked, underfunded teachers find the space to build relationships with students, to get to know kids who come from unfamiliar backgrounds, support to recognize their own attitudes and beliefs?

I want to mention a couple more classroom dynamics before ending this chapter; they will show up again in my later discussion. Even though progressive educators emphasize collaborative learning, children in most schools, especially public ones, still spend most of the day learning alone. This individualization of pedagogy has several motivations. First, it allows for evaluation; how do you grade individual students when you have many groups working together at the same time and therefore can't observe in detail? That capitalist pedagogy privileges evaluative metrics is cause and consequence of both internalized and institutional individualism. It also is easier to manage kids made to read books or practice math or fill out worksheets quietly alone. Unskilled in group interaction, children set into collaborative learning groups are likely to have some conflict. In overcrowded classrooms, conflict intervention takes time that is already scarce; preparing kids for standardized testing requires adherence to standardized curriculum, often too loaded for the time allowed. If in addition teachers are unskilled in managing these clashes as constructive moments, then they instead lean toward avoiding them. Conflict avoidance is a cultural norm in mainstream United States, reproduced in schools as well as nuclear families.

Grading quantifies competition on a personal level as well. Everyone knows where they fall on the scale of smart-to-stupid. These designations, intended to quantify ability, become internalized. With strong emotional impact, they suppress motivation (a concern well debated in the education field, but not mysterious). Futures are predicted with more or less subtlety as interpersonal racism, grounded in institutional dynamics, reproduces systemic inequality.

At the same time, white kids occupying dominant identities come to an unquestioning belief in their superiority. If they measure above their peers of color, they also turn a keen eye to how they measure among their white ones. Few students avoid the teacher's red pencil. Correct and incorrect answers play into a dominant way of thinking, in binaries. To be wrong is to earn demerits; before long a wrong answer becomes internalized as a wrong character. "I can't do math." "I'm not good at writing." "Science is not for me." All these conclusions about aptitude are internalized as failings on a fundamental level of self. So not only are young people alienated from others with whom they must compete, but they become alienated from their own creativity and unique forms of intelligence. Smart-stupid becomes a binary; spectrums of different ways of thinking, learning, and creating are ruled out in the gradebook. At the same time, the decisions children make about their attributes serve to inscribe racial, cultural, and gendered identities, along with deep beliefs in rights and entitlement.

In the small worlds where most childhoods play out, comparisons tend toward the simplistic; nuance dwells in larger contexts than the young can access. Where do children have an opportunity to recognize themselves outside the narrow parameters of home and school? Not in unstructured play, confined to a frantic few minutes at school, converted into sports after school. Team sports do give kids an experience of collaboration, but only according to another rulebook. Here again, activity is bounded by competition: is our team the champion or the underdog? Kids' positions within a team combines with the fortunes of the team as a whole to add another level of self-consciousness about one's separate adequate or inadequate standing.

For some children, the structure of pedagogy creates a contradiction that is both meaningful and painful. One young person I know grew up in Trinidad. Living in a collectivist community and a multi-generational family, they had little experience of individuation until they were enrolled in an upper-class private school. There, for the first time, they encountered the instruction to "do it by yourself." To ask for help or seek to share skills was greeted with a reprimand. The contradiction between culture outside the classroom and inside it, they realized later in life, was a direct imposition of colonialism. In village India, I witnessed small children learning the alphabet by choral repetition. Every child's voice was joined with every other in reciting the required learning again and again. No lone voice was ever called out. My friend learned to distinguish themselves from the group, a disjunction laden with confusion and meaning; the children in the village classroom in India experienced cultural integrity as they moved from home to school.

Examples of how we imbibe the ideology of individualism, and along with it get sorted into identity categories that carry heavy meanings about rights and agency, proliferate throughout life. Almost every experience lived inside a particular social structure reinscribes the primary belief systems. How we think as well as what we think, how we earn livings or don't, how we come together in families and then experience them crumbling, how we fail to use conflicts as moments of change and growth, again and again we find ourselves cut off from others in simple and profound ways. In the United States, all these experiences are played out in a society permeated with inequalities of many sorts.

One of the first protests raised by children across the spectrum of race, gender, and class is, "That's not fair!" Early in life, we experience injustices perpetrated on us, most often (but not always) with good intentions. An older sibling gets to stay up late to watch a favorite television show. A sweet-hungry child is told, "No dessert before dinner." A friend's parents let them play on the sidewalk in front of the apartment building. Children know what rules constrain and direct them, and they don't always agree. But over time, we learn to accept that which we cannot change. If we were denied access to the color purple, eventually we might lose the ability to see the color purple. Told we're being made to eat foods we don't like, go to bed before we feel tired, pick up toys when we are tired and want to leave them for the morning, and on and on, as access to fairness eludes us again and again, eventually we lose the ability to see injustice. We are conscripted into acceptance of other injustices as well. "Accept that which you cannot change" is good advice if the thing truly cannot be changed. But what if it can? What if we are confused into acceptance such that we lose the ability to imagine change? What if we consent to a system that is unjust to others, and also unfair to us?

If we do consent, eventually the contradictions between what we experience and what we're told, the scar of alienation that grows day by day in that dissonance, introduces uncertainty to our grip on reality. Under the stresses of daily insecurity, time scarcity, overwork, discrimination, and more, we begin to feel crazy. And when we object, if we say no more, we're told we *are* crazy. After all, don't we live in the land of justice, in the best of all possible worlds?

If worldview is the pond in which we swim, and if that pond is actually a goldfish bowl where we are alone, looking out through the murk and glass at other worlds but unable to access them, then we may well sink into confusion and distress. In a social world of isolation and professionalization, where do we turn for help?

6 **Psychiatrizing Discontent**
Hard Landings on Soft Couches

Meet God, aka the plumber George. I met this modest white working-class man, this master of sacrilege in 1958, and he changed my life. He was a middle-aged patient in a psychiatric hospital in Massachusetts at the time, I a seventeen-year-old pre-medical student in a nearby university. I volunteered in the institution because I thought I wanted to become a psychiatrist. Instead, I became a radical.

Growing up, I was intrigued by the differences between my family's lifestyle and the rituals I observed in my friends' households. My sympathy was touched by the tensions I heard expressed by my fellow teens. I watched and questioned and consoled, wanting to understand the root causes of family conflict. The daughter of a revered physician, I decided early that I wanted to follow my father's professional path. I determined I would become a psychiatrist, never a mother and housewife like my own mother. My ambition was heightened by the fact that my father firmly opposed that goal. Medicine was no life for a woman who, he was convinced despite my protestations, would also someday become a mother. Moreover, he considered psychiatry to be bogus medicine; psychiatrists were quacks, a category he despised. Spiced with my endemic rebellion against every expectation placed on me, I set forth boldly on my path.

At sixteen, I left home for college. My campus sprawled across lovely Massachusetts hills only a few miles from a psychiatric institution called Metropolitan State Hospital. They too occupied a large campus. But on theirs, ugly brick buildings towered over narrow walkways, casting lethal shadows over anything agricultural. Two thousand souls lived there, housed in dreary wards, many of them for lifetimes with no prospect of recovery or release. A small group of us undergrads approached the administration with an offer to volunteer. We would come several times a week just to visit with folks, a small heart tap of kindness. The staff of psychiatrists, seven of them in charge of all those thousands, readily accepted. Our cadre of college students waded into seas of people, most of them untreated for decades. Stench of urine soaked the wards as silent people clothed in grayed shifts sat on straight-backed chairs lining long corridors. We tried to talk with people; most remained silent, but very slowly we developed conversations with a few and were horrified by their stories. They had been committed, ten, twenty, thirty years earlier, without voice or recourse, to lifetime imprisonment because of behaviors others found weird or threatening. We began to track down family members, to advocate for release. Don't tell anyone, but in a few cases, we simply left keys in obvious places. Certainly, no staff was paying attention; there was a handful of attendants for thousands of inmates.

I formed a friendship with George. A plumber in his ordinary life, he was committed to the hospital because he insisted that he was God. Many of the people I met incarcerated at Metropolitan State were working-class folks with unusual temperaments and histories of notable stress. George's story, as he revealed it to me in bits and pieces over months, told of financial insecurity, familial conflict, and his own history of feared and experienced parental incompetency—in his own childhood and consequently in the troubles of his own children. An acute-care facility had recently been created at Metropolitan State in one of the more modern buildings; psychiatrists were experimenting with brand-new psychotropic pharmaceuticals just entering the market, as well as with electroshock and insulin coma "therapies." George was on the case load of a psychiatrist who told me his fixation was unusual. "Many patients have the delusion they are particular saints, or even sometimes Jesus. But God? Haven't seen that one before." In once-a-week talk sessions, he repeatedly asked George whether he "still" believed he was God; George/God could not lie, repeatedly admitting he not only believed he was God but that he actually was. The psychiatrist tried out numbers of the new antipsychotic drugs, each with multiple untenable side effects. He gave his patient a course of ECT, electroconvulsive therapy. George emerged traumatized, dizzy, and with memory loss, but still God. As a last resort, the psychiatrist sent George to the experimental Insulin Coma Therapy unit where people were plunged into deep diabetic coma and revived at the brink of death—occasionally emerging with fried brains. I assisted in that unit, holding people as they convulsed, importuning the half-mad doctor in charge that this person or that needed to be revived immediately!

I suppose in today's idiom I too suffered secondary trauma. Trauma matters because it is an experience of powerlessness so severe, and often so embedded in the body that it leaves long-lasting scars of doubt and insecurity. I wondered why George didn't take the one route open to him to escape the torture: simply giving his doctor the answer he sought, that his mind was changed by all the intervention, and he now knew he was mortal like everyone else. To me, his imagined divinity made sense. Now and then, George escaped from the hospital, but he always came back. He told the shrinks he had no memory of these escapades, but he told me he was only going to his local pub for a few beers. I wondered why he returned, speculating that he left for the companionship (and alcohol) that represented the best part of his life outside, but that he came back because he didn't really want to go home, knowing how much there filled him with guilt and a sense of powerlessness. Perhaps he also believed he deserved the punishment. An unusually mild-mannered man, lacking the aggressive masculinity stereotypically "normal" for men of his station in life, he confessed to me secret and severe self-recrimination for his failures: to earn enough money, to parent his gay son in an "appropriately manly" way, and so on. To reverse his self-image by awarding himself a God-like omnipotence was understandable to me, a fanciful overreach to be sure but harmless and sweet. In our many conversations, I argued that his life circumstances gave him less power than he thought he had to make everything all right for everyone in his life, and therefore less responsibility or need for guilt. Eventually George decided, with my encouragement, that there was justification for God to lie and told his tormentors he knew he was not really God, that it was only a wish. "I've got too much to do for one thing," he told me. "It's spring and I need to be out of here to make the grass grow—that's a lot of work."

On the day when he was scheduled to leave the hospital, I made a point of being present for a final meeting with him. "This place is a battlefield," he told me, "psychiatrists against patients. I'll make sure the doctors end up in hell. But you and I are going to share a beer at the pub in heaven someday." Moved and attuned to the political ideology embedded in George's sweet offer, I decided the last thing I wanted was to join the brotherhood (it was all male) of psychiatrists that so terrorized him and horrified me.

Shrinking a Population: Alienation and Oppression

George's experience lay at the intersection of two different forms of bodily control: one by imprisonment (in his case hospitalization), the other by pharmaceutical alteration of his mind and emotions. Add to that the cultural aspect. When normalcy is defined in linear ways, deviations become both fearful and infuriating. We must toe the line, and if we don't, and if our ways of deviating do not violate the law, then attempts are made to sweep us back into conformity through psychiatric means: medication and often also through its handmaiden, psychotherapy.

If the impositions of psychiatry were confined to a tiny portion of the population, we might be decrying abuse, or even oppression. But in the modern era, psychiatry's reach is far, far greater. In the last chapter, I sketched dynamics within "normative" families—that is, heterosexual, middle-class, and mostly white—that land people, saturated in a belief that their travail is their own fault, into so much distress that they turn to medicalized practices for help. Today, the National Institutes of Health estimates that one in five American adults has a diagnosis of some sort of mental illness. The greatest number of these are diagnosed depressed, with anxiety the next most common. Almost half of adolescents are considered to have a mental disorder, half of those labeled "serious."[1] If "mental illness" were instead a physical illness—say, Covid-19—it would be called a pandemic and there would be no debate about its socially located nature. As a culture, most people who are so diagnosed robustly dispute any causation other than that lying within their own genes, misdeeds, or other individualized fault. European statistics are not hugely different. Just before the Covid pandemic began, the relevant agency of the European Union estimated that one in six adults was diagnosable. Depressed women formed the largest cohort.[2]

For many years I've offered counseling and conflict intervention services influenced by a school of theory and practice called Radical Psychiatry, or sometimes Radical Therapy depending on how provocative we wish to be at the moment: none of us is a psychiatrist by medical legitimization. The word "psychiatry" is a composite of two Greek concepts: soul + healing. That, we contend, is the business of us all, not the exclusive province of those credentialed in a Western medical system. A foundational premise of the work is that people are both good and sane. To start from opposite assumptions is to foreclose the possibility of proving that people are indeed sane and good. Needing a way to describe the distress people come to us to help relieve, we adopted and revised a Marxist concept of alienation. Karl Marx had his analytic eye on alienated labor: the value produced by the efforts of working-class people that accrue not to their benefit but to those who own the means of production: the tools and raw materials utilized by workers to create commodities. Radical Psychiatry theorists theorize that alienation in lived human experience manifests as the unhappiness that is so prevalent, and that "professional" shrinks define as mental illness. The theory distinguishes three components, all of them interacting with each other to produce severe emotional distress: oppression, mystification, and isolation.

We are all oppressed. That blanket statement grounds everything else. By oppression, I mean that we exist in a world of coercion. Left to our own wishes and devices, we might all be artists and dancers, philosophers and magicians, gardeners and builders—exactly the talents most charming in very young children. But from an early age, we experience imposed limits, not only to what we are allowed to do but also to how we are allowed to think.

One brilliant night in San Francisco, as we lingered over dinner with our son and his family, three-year-old Mia wandered onto the deck and gazed out at the sky. A full moon rose, sharply sketched against the starry sky. I joined her at the rail.

"I want it," declared our acquisitive granddaughter.

"What do you want?" I asked, eager to satisfy her every wish: grandma's prerogative.

"That!" Her tone declared me an idiot as she thrust her finger toward the glowing orb.

I started to explain about planetary objects, distances, and a collective right to the moon when she interrupted.

"No! I want it. Get it for me."

I debated with myself briefly. Was it my responsibility to educate the child, or perhaps to correct her demanding manners, to oppress her acquisitive elan? But then I realized that, if I let myself, I too might wish to possess that luscious moon. Wouldn't most people if our fancies and our openness hadn't been, somewhere along the path to adulthood, been squelched. I decided to play along.

"How do you think we can get it? Maybe make a lasso?"

Delighted, Mia cast about for something with which we could lasso the moon, fastening quickly on a long dog leash lying by the door. We made a loop and set about casting it off the rail of the deck. Again and again, we failed in our mission—with increasing hilarity. Eventually, as the fun grew thin, I gave Mia some astronomical facts, only marginally interesting to her as she moved along to her next adventure.

What I did not do was tell Mia that her claim to the moon was wrong or foolish—or pathological. I did not discount what seemed to me a charming desire for something so beautiful. I stepped outside my science background and saw the moon as small and attainable, just as it was from the perspective of an enchanted three-year-old.

How many opportunities there are for grownups to impose our needs, our beliefs, our internalized rule books on youngsters. Our own imaginations oppressed by all we've had to sacrifice to become adults, we believe it is our responsibility to parent kids as we were parented. In one sense, we are preparing children to be obedient to coercive conditions over which, we assume, they will have little or no control. Soon, newborns will be schoolchildren. They will have to sit still, to solve problems in the way they are taught instead of the way their creativity directs them, and to occupy time as dictated by the school clock. Soon after they have submitted to these oppressions, they will enter the workforce. Few if any people are marched to the factory floor or the office at the point of a gun. The gun is instead internalized; we consent and do it to ourselves.

Lies and Isolation: Obscuring Oppression, Locking in Alienation

What locks in submission is mystification. We're told we live in the best of all possible worlds. We're told that happiness resides in a degree from an Ivy League college and a professional job in a prestigious organization. We're told that the economy is flourishing even while we are unemployed and can't afford the price of eggs. We're told that our leaders are looking out for our interests even while they amass huge fortunes, and we pinch pennies. Lies begin at home and metastasize in the public culture. We are a happy family, even when we are not. You are a bad child when you won't violate your morning body timing and hurry, hurry, hurry to get dressed so I can get you to school and myself to work. Once at school, the lies compound as teachers teach to prescribed curricula that censor certain politically inconvenient realities. Media further and constantly promulgate untruths, selling products based on fantasy and reporting slanted news. Ordinary people go to war defending their particular sources against conflicting versions passionately subscribed to by others.

If we had access to crucial truths—that there are plenty of resources to go around, for example, that they could be equitably shared, that selfishness is not natural and well-being is actively undermined by the structure of work, that cities could be built, if we had a collective will to do it, so that good housing became accessible to everyone, and on and on—then we might not blame ourselves for the multiple scarcities we face. But truth lies behind a secure wall because instead of seeking it, we blame ourselves. Having bought into the inevitability of individualism, we are frightened to admit to others how scared we are, how much we lack, how deeply we doubt ourselves. So we keep silent, ensuring the hegemonic fog in which we collectively wander, blinded and confused.

But consent to oppression is weakened when people honestly compare notes. "You mean you hate starting school so early in the morning as much as I do? Let's go on strike!" In the "normal" course of most lives, we do not share with others that we suffer. In a way, Facebook, with its endless pictures of happy people doing happy things with happy friends and family members, is an apt representation of the rulebook for social intercourse: keep a happy face to the world; don't air dirty laundry in public. Shame keeps us silent, and silence closes off all ways to discover how right, dignified, and worthy we are.

In these ways, oppression, mystification, and isolation lock us into the deprivation we might otherwise overcome. They also constantly reinscribe the great lie that we are all alone. To be without allies, to have nobody to whom we can turn in times of trouble, to be convinced that the fault lies in ourselves, not anybody else, not only makes us compliant; it also makes us crazed. Where we turn for help, to a therapist or psychiatrist, is another source of mystification. Mental health services rely on a fundamental premise that the fault lies in ourselves, not in the culture. Here, too, even as we talk with another human being, we are isolated by rules of confidentiality, suggesting that what ails us is a private matter, carrying risks of vague danger should it be shared. At the heart of isolation lie power differences. In the shrink's office, we face a living confirmation of our inferiority. Therapists do not reveal their own doubts and insufficiencies. They are carefully trained to keep themselves out of the conversation, except perhaps in carefully calibrated bits and drabs.

And so, even as we seek "healing," we are reinfected with an experience of inequality, mystification, and isolation.

I'll have a lot more to say in the final chapters of this book about how people can—and in different ways sometimes do—escape these interlocking conditions: building communities, embracing multiculturalism and accessing different worlds, taking action to change the facts. Before moving on, I want to highlight one other aspect of the psychiatrizing of discontent: how individualism, the victim trap, and deep internalization of racism go hand in hand.

Individualism, Mental Illness, and Powerlessness

Individualism, as I've said, uniquely characterizes advanced capitalist societies. That is not to say that there were not similar strains in earlier epochs or in other more collectivist societies today, especially among elites, nor variations in degree from one capitalist land to another. In modern America there are distinct features of the belief that each of us is alone and essentially responsible for our own fates. We blame ourselves for our problems, but on the other side of the equation we fail to see how successes, both ours and others', are built on the shoulders of many others. In our scientistic environment, we're taught to think in straight lines and isolated categories, not in flowing dynamics and interrelationships. At its extreme, individualism leads us to believe that we make our own reality: *there is no there there*. Gertrude Stein referred to her home in Oakland, but her eloquent phrase fits with the ultimate denial of history and context to which Americans are vulnerable, especially those most immersed in the dominant culture, primarily white Americans.

Two things follow: first, the very worst charge to be made against us is that we're victims or powerless. And second, if each of us is responsible for our own reality, then inequality is our own fault—or in a perverted twist of perception, the fault of the one who is oppressed. We blame the victim.

I often hear people whose struggles quite obviously result from reduced opportunities, inadequate educational resources, confinement to violent neighborhoods, and so on, resist the idea that they are victimized by racism, sexism, classism, or any other ism. In the previous chapter, Eladio's explicit emphasis on his resilience speaks of protest against any view of him as a victim, even while he appeared relieved when I suggested he had in fact been *victimized* by racism. This confusion of victimization and victimhood equates a quality in the person with external oppression. Victimization often generates resilience, resourcefulness, and the force behind both those capacities, community. People whose well-being relies on coming together with others stand a better chance of resisting the cultural and institutional forces imposed by the dominant culture. "I am not a victim!" is a declaration of fortitude and hope. The antidote to alienation, as radical therapy defines it, is just that: breaking isolation by building community, defying mystification through honest communication, and, fortified by such truthful relationships, taking action to change oppressive conditions.

But if people don't see community as an option, if the pace of life, the pressures of money, the overwork of jobs and home keep people too busy and too exhausted to do the additional work of accessing community, then isolation compounds mystification and keeps us subject to oppression. So many factors add to the difficulty of reaching out. The structure of cities, for example, impedes access to people with whom we otherwise have affinity. If you live in Oakland, it's very hard to make functional community with a dear friend living in San Francisco. Traffic, the cost of gasoline, the hardships of public transportation, all conspire to keep us isolated.

So when you're in desperate straits, when you feel depressed, find yourself blaming yourself for whatever problem of modern life confronts you, do you call on friends for help, knowing that they too are too busy and too pressed by their own life problems? Or do you call your therapist? When you do call your therapist, how much farther are you from imagining a better life? Or believing in your right and your ability to access or build it? When I counsel people or work with them in mediation—or what my wise colleague John Paul Lederach prefers to call "conflict transformation," a process that brings about not just resolution but change—the most effective thing I do is to imagine how different things might be in a hypothetical beloved community. What if this family had enough money to truly support them? What if this mother were raising children alongside her four best friends? What if this man facing daily microaggressions at his job and overlooked for the fourth time for a promotion that went to a less-qualified white colleague, what if he worked someplace where he was truly seen, valued, and rewarded? What then would become of the "symptoms" these people experience? The stresses and disappointments and insecurities they must overcome every day remain, but to be freed from the self-blame opens avenues for taking collective actions that may well help a lot more. To ask these questions is not to solve their real problems but to create a productive context for seeking change by rejecting a thick web of assumptions trapping people in isolation and psychiatric diagnosis.

This circular process—a society that produces a problem and then defines that problem as flaws of the individual—very effectively counteracts any possible revolutionary impulse. Why protest if you can't win? How even to imagine revolting if you are convinced that looking outside yourself for causation is an excuse? If you can choose to feel differently or at least choose to pop a pill that makes you feel better, then your failure to do so is another sign of moral failure, or perhaps another symptom of mental illness. When two friends, locked in competitive combat with each other, recently approached me for mediation, I asked how they defined the central conflict between them; each declared the other to have psychiatric problems. What then is to be done? There is no savior save the shrink or the prescription, no change for each friend to make, no real solution to the real differences and problems dividing them.

And so psychiatry becomes a political force, undermining rebellion and securing the centrality of individualism by constantly recreating that core definition of self. Psychiatry and its more secular version, psychotherapy, are the perfect consumer industries. More often private pay than publicly funded, practitioners never work themselves out of the need for their services. That is because their mandate is to treat human distress, and distress is the constant by-product of a society with inequality and acquisitive self-interest at its core.

The medicalization of these dynamics flows from and compounds an underlying characteristic of cultures based in capitalism: ways of thinking in categories, binaries, or straight lines. Mia's enchantment with the moon could never have happened had her three-year-old mind been deprived of magic. I believe she knew all along that the moon could not be captured, but that knowledge easily coexisted with another form of knowledge: that she could pretend, she could play, she could act as if, she could fail with joy. When the very forms in which we think are colonized by a society that controls our access to well-being, then empathy and fantasy become revolutionary acts.

Ways of Thinking
In Twos, Tens, or Rainbows

The enterprise of psychiatry depends on categorization, in this domain called diagnosis. The diagnostic manual (DSM-5-TR) offers clinicians lists of "symptoms" gathered under particular diagnostic labels. This process mimics medical diagnosis. If I have a sharp pain in the left side of my chest while also feeling faint; if my skin suddenly turns pale and pasty; if I can't breathe; then that collection of phenomena strongly suggests an organic event taking place: a heart attack. Recognizing this particular confluence of events may save my life, for it urgently dictates a course of action: rush to the emergency room. Once there, particular tests—EKGs, CTs, and other kinds of scans and blood tests—will confirm the diagnosis or send the doctor hunting for a more useful diagnosis through more testing. Confirming a diagnosis starts a patient along a well-trodden path of treatment.

In the psychological realm, however, no such orderly procedures exist. Empiricism fails; there is nothing to test or measure. But the label itself has multiple forms of force. It becomes a permanent part of the medical record, something with potential consequences legally and for employment. It is very often followed by the prescription of medications, powerful pharmaceutical substances that alter mind and emotion. It becomes a cell in the huge organism of capitalist profit generation: antidepressant medications yielded profits worldwide of $18.7 billion in 2024. Economists predict steady growth in these sales over the next decade "largely fueled by increased mental health awareness and rising demand for effective treatments for depression and related conditions."[1] Beyond all these measurable consequences, self-definitions are also altered. A sociological theory called "labelling" demonstrates how much we embody roles assigned to us. How often I have new clients introduce themselves with their diagnosis: "I am depressed/anxious/bipolar." In reality, these people may feel sad or frightened, but they are so much more than that. Just as the Black student in Little Rock accepted a self-definition of "not smart," which closely aligned with his perception of Blackness because, looking around, he could see that most of his African

American peers were also seated in "not smart" classrooms and therefore classified in a racialized category.

This diagnostic way of thinking and its intrusions into the psyche is only one example of the many ways cognitive function is structured by categorization. Staying in the medical realm for a moment, think of specialization: my spouse and I see a dozen different doctors for different parts of the body. The dermatologist who tracks skin cancer never speaks to the orthopedist who performs hip replacement, and neither has any contact with my primary physician except through the bureaucracy administering insurance. Suffering pain in her shoulders, Mariah was poked and prodded by practitioners specializing in disorders of the shoulders, producing no relief. Only when she saw someone specializing in pain management and therefore attentive to the experience rather than the isolated body part did she get treatment for the locus of the problem: her spine. Separating pieces of the body overlooks systemic causes of distress.

When we study science, we focus on physics or chemistry or biology, but rarely on the dynamic relationships among all three. We learn mathematics through rote practice, performing calculations labeled algebra or geometry or calculus but rarely related to each other. Students are tracked into gifted and not-gifted; what about the child who loves music and might easily relate it to math but who struggles with each subject when they're severed from each other? I know a young boy who had trouble memorizing the alphabet. By the age of six he already declared himself "not good" at English. His parents and his teacher drilled him daily, to no avail. A natural athlete, he expressed total joy when allowed to run around on the playground. Knowing how kinesthetic he was, a friend chalked a hopscotch diagram on the pavement, drew letters in a random order on the squares, and invented a game: "Jump to A. Now can you jump as far as B?" By Z, tired but joyful, he could recite the alphabet. Great teachers know how to escape the common practice of dividing knowledge into separate categories. In second grade, my son's teacher noticed that all the kids brought ugly little dolls called trolls to class with them. Banished by most teachers, the trolls remained poorly hidden in their desks. "Bring them out," invited the teacher. "Let's create a troll society." For the rest of the year, he taught math by setting up troll shops and setting the children to do troll business, English by writing and reading stories about trolls, art by building troll villages, history by populating stories about humans with troll substitutes, and so on. All those activities not only brought organic coherence to the interplay of the various subjects, but they also required collectivity. So much of conventional schooling insists on individual work: how else can students be graded and compared with each other? Not least importantly, the year of trolls made school so much fun we had zero power struggles in the morning about getting to school on time.

Good, Better, Best: Competition Infecting Cognition

Categorization lends itself to the second characteristic of normalized cognition under modern capitalism: competition. Once reality is arranged in discrete pieces, it can then be—and in almost every context, is—rated hierarchically. Certain modes of thinking rank higher than others: science more than art; counting more than conceptualizing; detail more than context. Most of all, people are ranked. For most children, competition begins at or near birth. Sibling orders become laden with comparisons. Families apportion characteristics as if only a finite number exist. My mother joked that her parents so often said that she was the pretty one and her older sister the smart one that she concluded that she was stupid, and her sister decided she was ugly. I got artistic and mathematical, my sister sweet and good caretaker. We, too, figured out the obverse attributes and accordingly internalized self-doubts.

Industrial production requires categorization at the same time that it requires specialization. The assembly line is designed to break tasks into measurable pieces that can be organized in a linear fashion: first this widget, then that screw, next this gear. But in reality, all scientific discovery at some point involves enormously creative acts of context and synthesis. Every hypothesis is a product of intuition built on knowledge of past discoveries but leaping forward through imagination. Nonetheless, science is taught and defined in modern capitalist societies as manipulation of quantities and materials, of things that can be counted and conclusions that can be proven.

People too need to be counted. In *Seeing Like a State*, James Scott lays out the progression of state power from tithe-gathering to population control.[2] The former could be accomplished through feudal relationships with collective entities. But the latter requires a countable relationship between the state and individuals. The decennial census becomes crucial: if government doesn't know who is where when, then control of tax collection, criminality, distribution of resources like education and voting, and so on, becomes impossible. In lands where migratory communities were once common, in South Asia, for example, permanent settlement was imposed by the imperial state. I saw firsthand in India the consequence of distribution of land to individual tillers. Where once farming was rationalized through the sharing of communal property, now each tiller "owns" tiny holdings, often scattered across territory intermixed with other people's land, difficult to irrigate and inconvenient to tend. Shortly before I moved to north India, the Japanese government had supplied small tractors to farmers in our area north of Calcutta, a gift from a generous rural development project. These cunningly designed shiny tools might well have been transformative—except nobody calculated the difficulty of maneuvering them on plots of land too tiny for them to turn. Nor could they be moved from one field to another without traveling over other planted fields belonging to other farmers. I saw tractor-carcasses, idle and rusting, scattered across the countryside.

Tidying Reality into Singularity, Losing the Power of Contradiction

Right along with the transformation of complex realities into discrete, countable, categorizable things, the organic dynamism of nature is transformed into something static. To be counted, reality must stand still. Straight lines supplant spirals. Nature is filled with curves: why do artists paint mountains, horses, women, clouds, and waves? Because all are curves, and all move—even mountains viewed through the shifting shadows of the cooling day. The idea that reality can be both this thing and that thing all at the same time is supplanted by the insistence that things either are or are not one way.

As a mediator of conflict, my major contribution is often to say, yes, you are right—and so are you. How two estranged people put together a picture of an event is commonly through contestation: "It happened this way!" "No, that's wrong. This is how it really happened." This familiar form of controversy so often evolves into "You're lying!" "No, you are!" Finding the larger narrative that makes sense of disparate perceptions and actions can break through absolute oppositions. But that is rare when people are trapped in competitive, alienated forms of consciousness. Competitive assumptions compound an inability to believe in multiple realities. "I must be wrong if you are right" bolsters a determination to fight for one's point of view rather than to seek the larger context that brings this version and that one together into a common story.

All these aspects of cognition—separating countable things into discrete categories, arranging them in a linear fashion, excluding a context that allows for things to be both-and instead of either-or—ensure acceptance of individualism. It is very different from the ways we explored the world as young children. Lucy felt her body and saw it in the mirror and accepted both as different but real. Adi queried Shelby's emotional response to living alone through a holistic process of comparison with no attached valuation. Her reality was neither better nor worse than his; it was simply different. He engaged in a creative process of imagining himself feeling lonely if he were to live in her circumstances, a sad emotion. Further, believing her word, he may have wondered why, if living alone did not make her sad, she nonetheless did seem sad to him—a recognition of a missing piece of information since we were protecting him from the dreaded word "cancer," the thing that made us adults sad. Both children's processes involved comparison *without valuation*, organic connections without categorization, transitions from physical states to emotional ones and back again, and many other forms of organicity. As we grow older, we are trained out of complex, contextualized thinking like this. Industrialization mechanizes cognition right along with production processes. In turn, the capacities we lose inhibit our ability to see through the mystification of oppression that underlies emotional conditions categorized as psychiatric.

And once diagnosed, having accepted a description of our distress that places solutions in external sources—therapists and drugs, whether of the pharmaceutical or street variety—we become increasingly ill-equipped to challenge the socio/political structures that in fact are at fault. Among these are the "isms": racism, sexism, classism, ableism. Structures both institutional and internal, social and psychological, combine to keep us compliant to cultures that do far too little to satisfy the full complex of human needs. We turn against each other, blaming those we see as privileged, and we miss the ways we too are oppressed. When we consent to silence that primal cry— "It's not fair!"—we consent not just to injustices done to those of an identity different from our own, but also the injustices we unwittingly suffer.

Replacing Tidy, Teleological Organization with Messy, Multicultural Collectivity

One way these limitations of cognition enforce racism is in a competitive ranking of different cultural styles. When I began to collaborate on a project with two colleagues I respect and admire, Mary Adams Trujillo and SY Bowland, both African American, each highly educated in a different academic field, I proposed we begin with an outline of what we intended to include in the finished book. All three of us mediate conflicts of one kind or another, and we shared a deep-felt critique of the racism we saw steadily shaping the growing professionalization of conflict resolution. Until recently something your grandmother or community elder or minister or older sister did, now mediation was becoming a fee-for-service practice. Professional services require regulation, and regulation requires a shared body of knowledge that codifies standards of practice. We watched with trepidation as a new "conflict literature" poured out of the universities, written mostly, given the racially and gender skewed academic demography, by white men. Our project was to produce a literature for the field written from lived experience by people whose practices and ways of thinking we could see were severely underrepresented. After several years of supporting people to write, we found ourselves ready to look toward publication. So we decided to assemble an anthology.

None of us had ever undertaken such a huge project; we pondered how to get started. Mary, a poet and ethnographic scholar and a trusting soul, proposed we simply put out the word inviting people to submit whatever they wanted. "What comes to us will tell us what the important themes are that organize the book," she suggested. But I thought we needed to give more direction from the start. I worried that we'd have to judge some submissions inadequate and seed competitive divisions. Better, I thought, to control the process more closely, setting guidelines and requirements in advance.

So SY and I took on the task of launching that process. I assumed she and I would share ideas and end up with an initial outline of the book we intended to compile. Then we'd identify writers and assign them topics. To my alarm, SY had a very different idea, not quite Mary's but closer to hers than mine: "Let's convene a phone gathering of mediators of color and ask *them* what they want to see in an anthology." I remember the sharp charge of anxiety I felt. Opening up the process at the very beginning, I worried, could produce chaos and conflict.

But I love and trust SY. So I gulped and said okay. SY quickly invited some fifteen people representing a wide range of identities and types of practice to a conference call. As I remember it, soon after the conversation began, an African American woman, a highly regarded employment mediator, remarked with a laugh, "You know that stuff they teach you, all that getting to yes stuff? Separating the people from the problem?" Laughter streamed across the phone line. "I don't do that shit," she said. "It's not going to fly with the people I mediate. So when we get in a room and close the door, I do something else entirely."

Stories rolled out as people shared what they thought of the formal methods they'd been taught. For the next three months, once a week the group continued a conversation laced with laughter, new people hearing about it from friends, and joining in. The stories were rich and raucous and searingly critical of the "white" approaches to our shared work. I thought of a concept by James Scott. He writes about "hidden transcripts," the stories marginalized people tell each other in private but keep secret from the dominant community that oppresses them.[3] In my study of school desegregation in Little Rock, one elderly Black man mentioned "complaining down by the big gate."

"What does that mean?" I asked, mystified. He told a story of two men working on the plantation. One says to the other, "I told the big boss exactly what I thought of him. Boy, did I tell him off!"

"And you survived?" exclaimed the other.

"Sure, here I stand."

The second man went off and soon after reappeared, bloodied and battered. "I told the big boss what I thought of him, and look what happened," he complained.

"*Where* did you tell him?" asked the first man.

"To his face, I stood right up and told him to his face."

"Oh, well, I told him down at the big gate."

I felt privileged to be hearing these stories "down at the big gate" and knew that our job in publishing the anthology was to bring them forward "right to his face." All knowledge-making is an exercise in confronting power.

At the end of a couple of months, we not only had an outline, but we also had writers. And they were writers who had what all writers need, whether we acknowledge it or not: support. They had bonded as a group. Writing is at heart a conversation. To wait until the end of a long, lonely process before you engage with an audience is torture—so much so that many people with so much knowledge to share simply never do it. Even with support, some people felt barriers so high and deep to writing, the trauma of the teacher's red pencil, that we instead recorded conversations with them, capturing their wisdom in transcribed form.

For me, a competent white writer and teacher, the lesson I learned was life changing. Not for the first time, I understood how deeply ingrained my assumptions were, and how one-up competitive: my way of thinking was the one right way. SY's way released control where I might have clasped it tight. Her way of thinking, always expansive, always relational, always grounded in a story, proved a whole lot more fun as well as productive!

If you want to read that book, it's called *Re-Centering Culture and Knowledge in Conflict Resolution Practice* (Syracuse University Press, 2008).

As adults, where are we allowed to deviate from empiricism and to base belief on faith and story and mystery? Religion is one place where the strictures of "knowing" only through what is scientifically verifiable are loosened. At the same time, in today's world, religion is paradoxically also one of the primary places where hierarchy—a linear ordering of power— and competitive patriarchy are most evident. In the next chapter, I want to tease apart the paradox of religion: source of spiritual solace and community, source of dehumanization through authoritarian absolutes and competitive certainties.

8 **Politicizing Empathy**
Alienation and Suffering

Today, I sit at my desk and write a book; you read these words at some unknowable time in my future, which will be your present. Today is a time when whiteness boldly claims dominance and male power rules. Critics of this reality face punishment on a daily basis; peril lurks around so many corners. For the writer of something the length of this book, another type of peril looms as well. Sterling insights of today could easily be made irrelevant or foolish by the time of publication, upended by the catapulting actions of a drama-addicted polity. If this space between writing and reading were a river, I'd be in the rapids right now, with no way to know whether calm waters lie ahead or Niagara Falls. So I hold on tight to my flimsy raft, discipline my emotional responses to daily injustices flowing from Washington, and try to use the immediacy of today to understand something under the surface of the fast-flowing waters: the rocky river floor and the canyon walls that shape and compel the dramas of these times.

The hallmark of these early days of the second Trump administration is an aggressive attempt to wipe out any progress toward equity and social caring made in the time before, scant as that progress had been in earlier twenty-first-century presidencies. Even administrations thought to be more progressive, those of both Biden and Obama for example, also deported people and restricted immigration. Neither boldly enabled social spending that might make a serious dent in economic opportunity. What is the peril to those in power of welcoming to "the land of the free" marginalized populations: people of color, women, newcomers from other parts of the globe, trans folks, people with disabilities, and others who are vulnerable to exclusion and persecution? Clearly, given the amount of wealth concentrated in the very top stratum of American society, it's hard to see these "outsiders" constituting much of a threat.

To insist that no uplift is needed for marginalized categories of people upholds a strict reading of individualism in the context of the American myth of meritocracy: if every individual has equal access to opportunity, then we are already all equal. Neither history nor sociology matters. It all rests with the capability and willingness of each of us to work hard. Social programs are irrelevant when you can pull yourself up by your bootstraps. If you insist on remaining imprisoned by your particular identity, believing yourself a victim of discrimination by those with privilege, well then, your failure to flourish is on you. After all, we can choose what we believe and what we feel; isn't that what our therapists urge us to believe?

These are all cultural tropes I explored in Part I that the Trump administration turned into harsh legislation on the very first day they took office. Their impact landed with particular force in three stark ways:

- On the day of Donald Trump's (second) inauguration, he banned all reference to race, gender, or other bases for identity other than "American," as if the very words used to denote diversity threatened some dreadful danger. Why did even the recognition of difference, even speaking its name, so challenge the purposes of those now in power?

- Present at that inauguration in positions of visual prominence sat the four wealthiest and most influential tech moguls in America, invited as a reward for enormous contributions they made to the Trump campaign. Why did they lend their financial heft to elect someone so morally questionable? Why did they bless his reign so visibly with their presence at the spectacle of his installation?

- Policies and executive actions flowing from the White House inflicted extreme hardships on many innocent people. What stands out is especially the cruelty of these actions, things like mass firings of federal workers; withdrawal of medical, housing and other forms of support for poor people; deportations of immigrants, stripping them of markers of identity such as hair and clothing, sending them to prisons in countries with no relationship to their places of origin; and so much more. What do acts like these say about the disconnect between the human beings inflicting them and those humans' own moral core, their humanity—about their alienation from self and others, and about ours?

I see the first two points, a confluence of identity politics and the extreme and mystified nature of class in America, as suggesting answers to the third. As we watch the Trump administration unfold, we witness a stunning drama of dehumanization in the casual way the president and his minions wield a pen to devastate lives, divide families, send people without process or recourse to brutal prisons, and so much more. Let's connect the themes I've touched on in Part I to look at how we can have come to such a heartless polity—and to its acceptance, often its celebration, by so many ordinary people, those of us without the power to enact dehumanized actions but only to look away or to applaud from the sidelines and hope we won't ourselves become the focus of this heartless attention.

How Institutions Unteach Empathy

When Adi exercised his empathic abilities to understand how he felt about his living situation, he used a facility I believe every young child possesses. We learn about ourselves and others by imagining others' realities and ourselves inhabiting them. Adi went even further; he based a new understanding of his own condition on his ability to feel himself into Shelby's existence. This capacity to empathize with another's reality is one of the most creative and important feats of imagination humans accomplish. We not only are able to understand the facts of another's life, but we can also write a vivid story of how it would be for us to inhabit a situation quite different from our own: to walk in another's shoes. What if I lived alone? How would my life be different from the one I'm living now in a household with two parents, a sister, and a very large dog? From birth, Adi was a child who was happy to be left alone. He could sit in the middle of the living room floor playing with a rubber ball, setting it off on a journey, following it and thrusting it on a new path. He both reveled in movement and could happily settle into contented stillness. So I imagine the question he asked himself—"How would I feel if I lived alone?"— was a genuine one. By extending his own experience of moments to himself into the new information about Shelby's household of one, he could play with how it might be for him, and he could voice a preference.

Perhaps Donald Trump was once a toddler filled with empathic imagination. Or maybe it is possible that he was born deprived of that ability, in the way that some people can't see certain colors. I suspect the capacity was hard bred out of him very early. But it doesn't really matter; what does matter is that without any apparent qualms as an adult he can inflict enormous suffering on other human beings, blink, turn around, and reward himself with gifted luxury airplanes, multi-million-dollar birthday parades, and plain old-fashioned boasting about his accomplishments. Some examples of the havoc he wrought in the first hundred days of his rule are:

- Thousands of immigrants kidnapped on public streets by masked men without official identification, sometimes chased through fields where they worked to grow the food that feeds America, and sent to prisons in other states to await deportation without process of review.

- Students, innocent of anything more threatening than critical comments in a university journal, confronted on public streets by masked men, handcuffed, and sent off to prisons in Louisiana and other places distant from their homes.

- Thousands of federal employees, career officials occupying their jobs for decades, summarily fired—and sometimes rehired shortly afterward only to see the departments they staffed dismantled, and their positions vaporized once again.

- Funding suddenly cut off for thousands of research projects, some at critical moments of completion, many close to producing new healing methodologies for agonizing conditions like sickle cell anemia, a genetic disorder afflicting primarily people of African heritage. But race was no filter for what programs were ordered dismantled. Research connected with cancer, birth defects, and a host of other conditions similarly met the hatchet.

- Wild schemes announced to annex Canada and conquer Greenland, declarations that agitated millions at home and abroad, distracting from an actual foreign policy choice to support Israel's war as it continued to eviscerate an entire population of Gaza, underwritten by state-to-state discussions about turning the seaside territory razed by continuous bombings into a Trump-themed resort.

With no whiff of apology for any of this heartlessness, Trump and his minions tore through due process, freedom of expression, balance of powers, respect for the judiciary, conflict of interest ethics, and other canons of the democratic process. Academic freedom lay tattered on the floor of the policymakers' parlors; universities were ordered to identify students and faculty protesting Trump policies and preferences, rendering them subject to life-changing punishment. Universities and public schools suffered withdrawal of huge sums of money, hamstringing both research and pedagogy. We the public witnessed with embarrassed horror images on the evening news of the leader of the nation, chastising and humiliating heads of state visiting from other countries.

When do little boys begin to tear wings off insects? Why do loving young daughters turn into mean girls, banning those their clique agrees to designate pariahs? When do freedom-loving Americans turn into enthusiastic followers of hate-spouting leaders with no human sympathy for those they injure?

Most of us have from time to time hurt others. We may step on toes without awareness, or sometimes even intentionally. Ignorance of what will cause pain to another is common. Indeed, it lies at one corner of the enduring structure of racism. What have come to be known as "microaggressions" are actions taken with little or no knowledge that they would impact the recipient adversely. When people of color say, "Ouch!" the most common response from white people is, "My intentions were good. I didn't know it would hurt you." Because of the complex dynamics of cross-racial interactions in our world, that response is often mounted with strong overtones of self-defense as well as undertones of guilt and shame. So exchanges like this go badly; that which is not overtly said communicates to the person of color on the receiving end that their experience is disbelieved. Perceived by the person who was hurt as a deflection of responsibility, this transaction is a wearily familiar call for forgiveness that chills whatever warmth a more equal human-to-human exchange might have evoked. Painful as these crossed encounters might be, they arise not out of a willful determination on either person's part to do harm. In ideal circumstances, giving voice to both people's experience can move beyond impasse to learning. Deeper understanding, when reciprocal, builds compassion, allowing for empathic understanding of what went wrong and how to remedy errors, as long as mistakes were made in ignorance, not intention.

Sometimes, however, there can be mal intent. Sadism—taking pleasure in the pain of others purely because it is pleasurable—I believe to be very rare. In all the years of working with people, some thousands of people whose histories and daily travails I've listened to over many years, I cannot think of a single individual I thought did harm to others purely to derive some sort of self-gratification. More often, when people come to learn they have inflicted pain on another, they feel remorseful, contrite, guilty. Shame may interfere with genuine apology; indeed, we may fight against the knowledge of the wrong we've done. But deep down, our own sense of moral integrity is wounded, and we seek to redress that injury to ourselves, and ideally to the other person as well.

If not out of sadistic pleasure, why do some millions of Americans continue to celebrate acts by their elected government that they might deplore under any other conditions? We know that people can be induced to participate in extreme violence in wartime and in frenzies of civil unrest. From everything I was told, the riot I uncovered in Bangladesh was extremely mild by comparison with the communal slaughter elsewhere a few years earlier, at the time of partition and independence. "A few young men exchanged blows on the side of the riot," one man reported. The "riot" itself was a sit-down event. (In the course of my writing about my study in a book called *Some Trouble with Cows*, a student questioned the word "riot," pointing out it seemed more a sit-down protest. Demonstrating how much colonialism infects the vocabulary of colonized people, I looked back at my interviews and discovered it was the only English word the villagers themselves had used.) There were some deaths, but people insisted they were inflicted not neighbor to neighbor but by the police who were called out to quell the "disturbance." I can't know whether these stories were sanitized so as not to incur my disapproval. A "European" stranger, some sort of authority, I was also accompanied by a person they knew well, who, as they also knew well, worked for a local development organization, a private group in control of significant resources with the power to dispense or withhold them. But assuming that the stories I heard were true in the main, even allowing for likely understatement ("There was some trouble with cows"), they spoke of restrained violence, a demonstration of opinion and intent rather than murder and mayhem.

That ordinary people can be induced to acts of extreme cruelty, however, is historically proven. In 1992, Christopher Browning published a book called *Ordinary Men*.[1] Using primary sources such as dry bureaucratic directives and later court testimony, Browning tells a harrowing story of how a group of middle-aged German men, judged too old for active combat, were sent to Poland and made to overcome their inhibitions as they carried out their orders to slaughter Jews. Organized into a police battalion with the assignment to take groups of people into the forest and shoot them, at first some refused. But as more and more of their peers fell in line, and plied with alcohol and exhortations to camaraderie, they soon took to the task with barely a backward glance. By their own testimony, they had no particular animus toward Jewish people. Anti-Semitic Nazi ideology influenced them only in a detached way, if at all. More horrifying than hatred, the work of genocide became normalized: all in a day's work.

This example of ordinary people turned lethal speaks to so many other historic cases: ethnic cleansing in Bosnia, genocide of Tutsi people in Rwanda, the massacre and starving of Palestinian people in Gaza as I write, to cite only a few of the many horrific instances throughout modern history. Most of us never experience what the men involved in each of these examples did (and do) on a daily, normalized basis. But we do share the experience as witnesses. Day after day, we see images in the evening TV news and occasionally on the front page of our daily newspaper (if we are among the few who engage with such artifacts of a past age anymore) of people suffering as bombs destroy their homes and slaughter their children in Gaza and in Ukraine. We may read an account that mysteriously breaks through the algorithm governing our online news sources of carnage in the Congo or starvation in South Sudan. But in all these cases, we often simply look away. Perhaps we shake our heads, grimacing at the ugliness of what we see. Perhaps these same physical reactions are evoked by the unhoused people we pass camped on the sidewalks beside the streets we travel to the grocery store or to work. What is that reaction? A mixture of disgust, recrimination, and perhaps fear that some such fate could befall us, too? Is there sympathy mixed in; if so, to what end? Do we feel moved to action, or do we duck our heads, feel our powerlessness, and move right along?

In a soon-to-be-published book, Mariah Breeding gives us stories of people brutalized in their youths by siblings—or brutalizing them. Entitled *They Looked Away*, she uncovers the multiple ways that parents, in their uncaringness or, more likely, their powerlessness and fatigue, failed to intervene. In the absence of intervention, however, they unknowingly taught their children to accept injustice, to expect no protection, to look away from other people's victimization in fear and futility.

And so along comes Donald Trump and we shake our heads and perhaps briefly protest his massive cruelty. We ask each other, "What should we do? Should we leave the country or fight? But how do we fight?" And we put the laundry in the washing machine, and we take out the garbage, and we prepare one more nutritious meal, and we look away.

I write these paragraphs not to blame any of us but to illustrate the pain of normalization. How often I've said that the first protest most of us engage in is, "It's not fair!" I said it when my older sister was allowed to do something I could not. You may have said it when you were denied dessert until you ate your peas. My son certainly said it when I told him he had to go to school because it was the law. We impose disagreeable realities on our children because they were imposed on us, and we don't know what else to do. Or perhaps we impose them because we've come to believe they are right and proper: "It's for your own good." But is it? Have we gained maturity, or have we drunk the Kool-Aid? What else do we come to accept as natural and right when we consent to the small things: fold your napkin when you leave the table. Put your dishes in the sink. Leave your muddy shoes at the doorway. All these things seem correct or inconsequential, but they form a pattern in our hearts and brains. Each is a template for accepting what we might otherwise question. Simultaneously, we accept a version of the world around us, of who we are and who is ours, of who is other, of who is entitled to the good things of life and who is not.

Belonging and Exclusion, by Whose Choice?

Among the most deep-seated things that become normalized is something people of Spanish heritage living in Northern New Mexico call *querencia*. My friend Roberto Chené introduced me to the concept over brunch recently. *Querencia* is the place one calls home. But it is more than home: it is a relationship to a land and a people, to cultural practices and particular adaptations of language. *Querencia* applies as well to a feature of Spanish bullfighting: the place in the ring where the bull feels most safe and makes his last stand. Ernest Hemingway described it in *Death in the Afternoon*: "It does not usually show at once, [*sic*] but develops in his brain as the fight goes on. In this place he feels that he has his back against the wall and in his querencia he is inestimably more dangerous and almost impossible to kill." *Querencia* is a place to dwell and a place from which to defend against perceived danger.

Roberto described *querencia* as a sense of place and of belonging. It is something he experiences, and I do not. Roberto is the descendant several generations down the line of people from Spain, France, and probably a few other places, finding a place in New Mexico. Roberto, a member of a Catholic order in his youth, left the church and married a lapsed nun after both left their orders for love and politics. Both carry with them a strong legacy of liberation theology, manifesting it in their lives in many ways.

I am the grandchild of immigrants from Eastern Europe. As a transplant from New York, even as I belonged to a Jewish community in Fort Worth, I turned away from that heritage in alienation from my fellow community members who witnessed racism in Texas and counseled silence, saying, "There but for the grace of god go we." As a teenager, I felt nothing but anger, unable to hear that sentence without thinking, "For that very reason, we must speak out!" When we meet for one of our frequent lunch dates, Roberto points out to me the places he lived in childhood, the spots where different moments in his eighty-year history took place. I moved to New Mexico six years ago. He knows *querencia* as a normal part of life, through a lifetime of belonging. I am the wandering Jew.

"Place" is a concept I heard often in my various research interviews. Alumnae from Central High School, for example, again and again expressed particularly sharp resentment about Minnijean Brown, one of the nine Black students enrolled the year of desegregation mayhem. I pressed people to tell me why they so disliked her; people were mostly unable or unwilling to put words to their feelings. But one woman, struggling to do so, at last burst out, "We were fine with them coming to our school. But Minnijean walked the halls like she belonged there." That insult to what my interviewee described as "just our way of life" was more than the white students were willing to tolerate.

I met a white woman living in the desolate Kansas village where I went on a quest to understand how people formulated political choices in the lead-up to a presidential primary. This woman offered me coffee and cookies in the house where she was born. With a distinct sense of pride, she told me this house was built by her great-grandfather and had been continuously inhabited by her family. Her friend who joined us for the conversation nodded appreciatively. "She went away for a while," she contributed, "but she came back."

"Yes. It was scary in the city where I lived. I tried it and didn't like it. Here, I know everyone. My kids ride their bikes everywhere and I don't worry."

Later in the interview, I asked whether anything scared her now. She thought for a moment. "When I get up in the middle of the night and I look out and a car drives by, if it's 3:00 in the morning—who is it and what are they doing there? Are they going to come back someday and rob us, or . . . you know?"

Startled that the existence she had so far described as peaceable and safe nonetheless could turn so frightening in the night, I asked, "Who do you imagine that robber would be?"

"I don't know," she said, her eyes shifting toward her friend. "I don't know. A stranger that comes through town."

Hemingway attributes the bull's search for *querencia* to the fight: " … develops in his brain as the fight goes on." I wondered who or what this ordinary woman in a Kansas village imagined she was fighting, who she thought intended to so harm her? Like the bull, humans seek *querencia* when our safety is threatened. This unidentified stranger defined the close-drawn boundaries of my interviewee's *querencia*.

A white woman living in a suburb of a large city described to me her fear of neighbors from a different land. "I'm a little afraid when I open the door and I see someone from India, or someone I'm not familiar with. Maybe that's what it is, I'm just not familiar with them, even though they live here, and I live here."

Each of these reflections of fear or discomfort with people defined as "other" came my way some years ago. Each person spoke to me in a managed way. I remember one Little Rock alum who, in the course of our interview, suddenly said, "What must you think about me? You must think I'm a racist. And maybe I am." Talking to another human being elicits self-consciousness; nobody wants to appear to be "bad" in the eyes of another. Today, however, my wife called my attention to a particularly egregious string of invectives on Facebook. A reel of an Islamic religious celebration on a New York street showed a large group of men chanting and moving in unison. At first, I thought Mariah was simply calling my attention to something pleasing in its simplicity, intensity, and collectivity. But then she changed the experience entirely.

"Have you looked at the comments?" she asked.

When I found the small icon to click, I found hundreds of them. One after another, feeding on each other as they rolled out of the internet like a poisonous avalanche, they called for the humiliation of the people portrayed. As hatred fed hatred, commentators called for them to be slaughtered by drones, by bombs, by tanks, and marauding automobiles. People insisted they could "smell the stink through my phone," reminded each other of 9/11, insisted The Big Apple be renamed The Rotten Apple. Calling on ICE (Immigration and Customs Enforcement) to arrest and deport them, they gleefully consigned them to a newly built detention center in a Florida swamp, named Alligator Alcatraz in cynical expectation of a grim fate for anyone who sought to escape.

Anonymity releases—what? Truth? The worst side of human alienation? It seems clear to me that whatever else is going on in this long, long diatribe by strangers is that a perverted form of *querencia* is being constructed. Each comment builds hatred greater than the one before. Each comment is a brick in a wall separating "us" from "them." How many of the people writing these awful things would actually march this group of celebrants to the forest and shoot them? How many wake up the morning after a virtual feeding frenzy like this and feel shame? How many celebrate the leaders who, with a wink and a nod—and sometimes with full-throated participation—let the evil genie out of the lamp?

And what does this outpouring of vileness communicate to anyone in the many categories of people who are defined by the white center of America as "other"? Several years ago, I was asked to mediate the leadership of a union. Their all-white executive group had recently been unsettled when a Black woman was elected to office, placing her on the leadership "team." The immediate conflict requiring intervention did not actually involve her; two white officers didn't play well with each other, interfering with urgent work needs. But as I talked with individual members of the group, many people expressed discomfort with the African American newcomer. She delayed talking with me for a long while, at the last moment expressing doubts about whether she would participate. As we finally talked, I asked, "Do you feel alienated?" Looking up in surprise, she snapped back, "Of course. This is America!"

Remembering this eloquent remark now, I wonder how many people actually do want *this* America. Even those swept along with the Facebook hate orgy, confronted with that question, might recoil. But meanwhile, there is a feedback loop animated, something we Jewish teens experienced in Texas. By a sort of unspoken agreement, we and the Christian kids kept apart. How often do multicultural associations fail, without an active conflict, without a word spoken, because a negotiation of belonging—of *querencia*— is always on the table, sometimes heavily loaded contextually with violence. We define the ways we share qualities and characteristics with others of our ilk. We honor the foods and colors and clothing that we value in common. We intuit the feelings of others toward us, toward our world, and we carry generational trauma of violence, heavily reinforced by current evocations. We feel alienated and seek the comforts of the known, turning away from the perils of unfamiliarity. White people in the mainstream do something similar, perhaps personified by the stranger who drives through town in the night or who moves in next door.

Querencia travels; displaced people may feel a strong sense of it toward the places their ancestors left. Perhaps part of what ails America is that so many of us have lost those links to our roots. Sometimes I ask people where their people came from; I'm always surprised how often they do not know. We are a population of the displaced, with only those few exceptions, Native Americans who somehow amazingly survived forced eviction from the lands of their ancestors. If *querencia* gives us a sense of safety, it does so through the dual benefit of sharing aesthetics with others and defining boundaries: you are in, you are out. Geography is not necessarily determining. What happens when the boundaries are lost, when people carry with them the disruptions of migration, when the national zeitgeist works against an ability to mourn our losses as well as celebrate our gains? Where do we turn then for solidarity? The farmers in Bangladesh turned to religious identity; the coeds in Little Rock identified racial belonging; many Americans choose both religion and race.

Losing the Power of Empathy

In each case, the boundary drawn constituted a limit not only to belonging but also to empathy. We *feel* those with whom we share identity; we have trouble finding that visceral connection when we don't. The stranger in the night is imagined to be dangerous; so too the stranger at the door even when we recognize her as a neighbor. At which point did the Germans in Poland stop seeing the Jews they slaughtered as human? In the concentration camps, there was a certain technological and bureaucratic distance between murderer and murdered, unimaginable and horrific as that distance was. But in Poland, the "ordinary men" performing genocide stood close before the women, children, and elders they shot, casting their still-warm bodies into pits to be covered with lime and buried. How do our eyes stop seeing our own limbs and faces and hearts in those we harm?

That we do stop is evidenced again and again. We are horrified as we witness a video of Derek Chauvin slowly asphyxiating George Floyd. But we look away when we pass by an emaciated homeless person, giving them only a glancing dismissal: "An addict, no doubt; brought it on himself." Or perhaps you or I have not grown such calluses over our capacity for sympathy yet, but still we drive by. We don't stop to help; we don't even stop to yell at the heavens, "How could this have happened?!" Why would we shout? What good would it do?

It is this combination of helplessness and belonging that keeps us in place, even when the place where we belong is one we decry and think about leaving.

If *querencia* is about belonging to a group of people with shared identity, it is also about belonging to a land and a history. Often, though, from the outside we misidentify people as having an identity in common, only to have some event reveal that identity is a plural noun. A prime example is a surprise revealed by the 2024 elections: the "Latino vote" for Trump. Even earlier, divisions among people broadly defined as Latino could be seen if we looked closely. There were Latinos storming the Capitol on January 6, 2021. Enrique Tarrio, the son of migrants from Cuba, headed the Proud Boys who led that assault. While Democrats won a majority of the 2024 Latino presidential vote, Republicans came close, getting about 40 percent.

That number seems highly significant until we begin to break down which Latinos supported Trump. What the available data suggests is that many were of Cuban or Venezuelan heritage. Both those countries saw large exoduses of their wealthier people when governments that championed the rights of the poor came to power. While class influenced Latino electoral support for Trump, no doubt there were also other migrants from Spanish-speaking lands who voted for him. It is not surprising when the second, third, and fourth generations of immigrants seek to protect what privileges they have achieved, competitively denying them to newer waves. That certainly happened among the Jewish people of my community in Texas. Not only were they shaped by the discrimination they faced in the new land, a less lethal echo of the anti-Semitic pogroms that massacred some of their ancestors in the old country, but they also faced many of the economic uncertainties that their Christian neighbors bemoaned as well. These children and grandchildren of immigrants from Eastern Europe and Russia survived as middle-ranking employees of companies that periodically swept out older, more costly workers, or they established small businesses or professional practices as accountants and lawyers. In other words, they were typical middle-class Americans, and, like their Christian peers, nothing was guaranteed to them beyond their own efforts. The Jewish community frequently stepped forward to extend a little aid to somebody in their midst in trouble, but significant help was not to be depended on. That some of them voted Republican, hoping that conservative fiscal policies might be beneficial to them, is not surprising. Why, then, shouldn't immigrants who happen to be Brown people do the same?

What these political cleavages within a seemingly homogenous identity group reveal, though, is the heterogeneity of even the most same-seeming communities. My closest Catholic friends, people like Roberto and his wife Connie, feel deeply that the Christian mission is service to the poor and others in need. Their theology goes well beyond the church door; they literally *feel* the distress of others. Empathy is core to their spiritual beliefs. There are other Christians, however, who explicitly preach the evils of such empathy. In 2025, a theology professor named Joe Rigney published a book called *The Sin of Empathy* (Canon Press, 2025). He argues a thesis in support of Christian nationalists, claiming that empathy is weaponized by people who consider themselves victims of discrimination. Focusing especially on trans people, he includes LGBTQ people in general, people of color, and others as well. Reading many opposing arguments by well-respected theologians and lay people, I've puzzled over the basis for these claims. Empathy would seem to be much in the same category as apple pie. Why would people who seek a society governed by fundamentalist principles of Christianity oppose empathy? A central example Rigney offers is telling: parents who are shamed into supporting their trans children by threats that they might otherwise commit suicide: "Better a live daughter than a dead son." Rigney argues that parents are terrified into a wrong set of choices by manipulation of their empathy for their children.

Internalizing Oppression, Losing Authenticity

I don't need to replicate here the many discussions arguing Rigney's points. Instead, this attack on empathy leads me to a deeper understanding of something my colleagues and I identify and work through with clients all the time: a distinction between "authenticity" and socially inscribed rules and prohibitions. I've written earlier about something I call internalized ideology; in the alternative therapy domain, we call it internalized oppression. I see the injunction to avoid empathy as a prime example of the dynamic. Which precise rule book we internalize depends very much on the type of society we live in and on our specific place in the social order. White girls, for instance, are heavily enjoined to be kind and helpful, precisely those attributes most relying on empathy. But these same powers are central for training to assume the social roles that enable isolated domesticity. Empathy looks outward, in the extreme eclipsing an ability to also look inward, specifically to recognize our own wants and needs. If your role model is a mother whose world is narrowed to home, and perhaps whose resentment manifests in troubled relationships with her daughters, you may at fifteen be questioning that assignment. I did, rebelling against my father's assumptions that I would become a wife and mother. Little wonder that some fifteen-year-olds, at a time of fierce resistance to social training, turn mean.

Boys, on the other hand, learn early in life, through sometimes particularly harsh transactions, to be "brave," meaning not to show fear or pain. That too requires a focus on others' view of you, not awareness of what you actually feel. Culture and racial oppression further tailor a balance between self-knowledge and social conformity. If you're Latina or Guianese or East Asian, you might be saturated by many forms of admonition and reproval that family always comes first, one's own ambitions a very far second. We've seen in an earlier chapter how in the 1980s Black male students in Little Rock internalized the message that they were not smart, while their counterparts in 2025 Pennsylvania instead identified themselves as criminals. Messages are local, temporal, culturally specific, and always compelling.

Both gender and race are heavily inscribed through the mechanism of internalizing judgment. My friend Beverlee talks about the consequence to her when Black adults described her child self as "high yellow" with "good hair," both physical characteristics bequeathed to her by some unknown white ancestor. Very possibly, this contributor of the genes that showed up in Beverlee's skin color and hair texture may have been a rapist, perhaps even the enslaver of her great-great-grandmother. What pain lives daily in being distinguished from others of one's community, in one frame compliments, in another symbols of differentness, an outsider both in the Black world and in the white one? I've earlier mentioned the many stories I've heard from African American boys raised in neighborhoods where everybody was Black, discovering racism only when they ventured out of their community for the first time at age seven, stunned and frightened when called names and bullied. If a central feature of your identity is connected by intractable threads to negative experiences—tightly curled hair or chocolate-colored skin—you are in danger of learning to think about yourself as ugly or existentially flawed. That's why the sixties slogan "Black is beautiful!" was so powerful. It challenged a derogatory meaning of particular physical qualities with a celebratory one. The Afro became a revolutionary symbol.

For women of all races and almost all appearances, how we look seriously impacts how we're valued by others and how we feel about ourselves. In all my years of counseling people, I never met a woman who didn't have some strong dislike of some part of her body. From birth and throughout life, most of us see signs and hear messages that tell us our bodies are imperfect. We take in with our daily bread messages that we are too large, a message that translates into "out of control" as we struggle to contain our appetites and deny the pleasure we feel in eating "fattening" foods. Even one model, tall, blond, thin—all the aspects of the "ideal female body"—hated her toes. "Look how curved the little toe is! I wish I could wear sandals, but I can't," she declared. Another woman desperately needed to change jobs. A highly regarded executive secretary, her skills would seem to guarantee she'd be snapped up by a new boss. But beautiful and confident in her capabilities though she was, she doubted her hireability because both medical charts and she herself defined her as overweight. "I need to lose thirty pounds before I can interview for jobs," she insisted. Size is a major and constant devil for women, and in more recent years increasingly for men as well. I've wondered whether weight became an issue for more men when women gained more traction in the labor market. The more challenged male applicants believe themselves to be, the more they may feel compelled by cultural standards of physical attractiveness.

Whatever specific message is involved, internalized oppression interferes with empathy. It is very hard to feel into another's reality when we cannot feel our own. We suffer alienation in many forms: from nature, from community, from other people, and from ourselves. With minds saturated in externally imposed standards and rules, we grow further and further away from an ability to sense, feel, name what we truly believe, want, need. Uncertain of our own reality, we adopt that which is depicted all around us, whether through media, authority figures in our personal lives, religious teachings, or authoritarian leaders. Morality becomes a learned matter, not an innate sense of what's good and right. It loses all context, becoming absolute and timeless.

Fat is always ugly, everywhere and always. Never mind that in hungry lands where people starve, fat means well-being. I remember the visit to India when I noticed the bellies of my friends from Punjab, beautifully bulging over the tops of their low-hung sarees, disappearing. Delicately, they waved away the delicious sweets so generously offered to visitors. Along with barbers and fruit sellers squatting on the sidewalks of New Delhi offering their services and wares, there now were bathroom scale-*wallahs*, men in possession of a bathroom scale who charged a few *paise* for a weighing. I understood that the global economy had now inflicted on urban India this painful feature of the global culture.

Two stories from my own life about the pervasive control "fat Pig" holds on women: when I was a young adult, my mother suffered a strangulated bowel. In sudden pain, she was rushed to emergency surgery where doctors removed a major section of her colon. I flew from India to help care for her during a very long convalescence at home. When I arrived, she was bed-ridden, constantly nauseous, vomiting frequently: a very sick woman, and she looked it. Within minutes of my arrival, she told me in a weak but gleeful voice, "I've lost twenty pounds! I just hope I lose more and can keep them off."

A parade of women came to visit. My mother was beloved in her community; the emergency illness frightened her many friends. Now, they came to wish her well and to tell her again and again how worried they had been, how unimaginable that they might lose her. As they commiserated with the pain of her convalescence, they extended convalescent gifts of gratitude: what they called "gooey desserts." Proudly, they offered the cream pies and chocolate cakes they'd mostly not baked at home but bought at a favorite bakery. My mother regarded them approvingly and offered them back, knowing sadly that she couldn't eat them—yet.

Food dominates and food oppresses when the measure of satisfaction is not hunger but size. As children, my sister was considered "overweight." Over what weight? I wondered. To me, she was just right. Indeed, my "obese" mother's size represented nothing to me but comfort. Cuddling on her lap, my head against her voluminous breast, was the very definition of nurturing. But my parents were determined that their daughters would not follow their footsteps down the path of fatness, and so we were both given a daily dose of Dexedrine, the drug of choice in those days for weight loss. Out of fashion for many years now, Dexedrine is speed. They wondered why my sister and I both suffered insomnia. Was it a mental affliction (although those terms were rare back then)? Despite the "side effects" (which were actually the chemical point of the drug), we continued to be given them throughout our childhoods. I was "pudgy," one of the many finely graduated terms to describe degrees of undesirable size. When at sixteen I left home for college, intentionally "forgetting" to take along the pills I was supposed to continue swallowing daily, I lost so much weight in the first three months that I was hospitalized as doctors searched for a pathological cause of my metabolic transformation.

Today GLP-1 has replaced Dexedrine. Many people I know are shooting up weekly with Ozempic or other semaglutides. Mostly, people are losing significant amounts of weight, although they also suffer frequent nausea and bowel problems. Some find ways to induce medical insurance to cover the cost; others scrimp to pay privately. What almost everybody reports is a profound relief from a constant inner focus on food: am I hungry? What should I eat? If I have the sandwich I want for lunch, how little will I have to eat for dinner? It's the mental affliction that these drugs seem to relieve as much as the weight loss that keeps people on them.

The particular standards and rules we internalize are not accidental; they are the carriers of particular cultures and social structures. Judgments about body size map social lines. If you know what an individual's internal dialogue is about these questions, you can guess that person's gender, race, class, and perhaps geographical place on the globe. Are the only alternatives for Black women to be seen as exotically sexualized when thin, "mammy" if large, the tough but endlessly nurturing mother enslaved to the wishes and demands of white children? The critical gaze of men toward women becomes internalized by women ourselves, and we turn it cruelly—competitively—on each other. Gay men, too, feminized in the distorted definitions of dominant culture, internalize standards of physical desirability that cast some in, render others subject to the fearsome perils of aging.

Class defines beauty. "The poor are plain, virtuous if humble and hardworking, but mostly ugly. Almost always ugly," wrote Dorothy Allison. In her complex memoir, she gives us a glimpse of the intersecting factors—rape, gossip, sexuality, and more, all carried through generations—that define her as ugly but smart, her sister as beautiful and also stupid. There comes a moment when they redefine themselves: "You are not stupid, and I am not ugly." That is a moment of protection for both, of respite from the oppression of self-definition imposed by community standards and internalized as identity.

Whether the voice is about food or success or love or whatever else, internalized standards intrude in our consciousness as negative self-talk. We chastise ourselves in the voices of our schoolers. The grammar of internalized oppression is absolute. "You are . . ." fill in the particular attribution: ugly, stupid, bad, sick, and so on. We are inundated with a constant stream of injunctions: "You should . . ." "You must not . . ." As we listen to these commands, the voice of our own common sense becomes dimmer and dimmer. Remember Adi sorting his desire to live with loved ones from Shelby's contentment living alone: his process rested on empathy, an ability to feel himself into another's situation, and also on context, a recognition of the larger circumstances influencing his life and Shelby's. Absolute injunctions stand outside time, circumstances, cultural specificities, or any other factors needed to lend depth and nuance to truth.

How Alienation Undermines Agency

What often gets diagnosed as mental illness is actually a manifestation of the human distortion wrought by alienation. When we live with a condemning internal voice ("You are fat/stupid/sick/bad/flawed in so many ways") that is compounded daily with a lived experience in the material world of barriers to happiness (too little money, too little time, too much to do, too much competition, too much conflict, etc.), then we lose life force as well as feeling. We become, quite literally, biochemically "depressed." Pop a pill and maybe feel a little better, but the conditions that interfere with well-being still continue, while self-blame depresses any belief in a possibility of relief. Finding comfort from others also becomes elusive because shame keeps us from speaking our truth to loving others—who themselves struggle with the same forces.

At each level of alienation, we lose agency right along with access to empathy and a capacity for collaboration with others. Agency requires solidarity; the lone individual changing the world by dint of superior leadership skills is a myth. If an ability to bridge differing ways of doing things is lost, how can we form relationships of respect and collaboration across social categories, especially when we are constantly told by so many manifestations of the culture that these divisions signify something real? Competition for the "right way" of doing things fertilizes cleavages, impeding creative shared work to co-create new realities. The unknown becomes mysterious and the mysterious threatening.

Meanwhile, as we lose access to our authentic truth, we also lose access to that primitive cry, "That's not fair!" But just as we fail to protest injustice toward others, we also become confused about how we ourselves are oppressed. Is it fair that the secretary had to shoot herself with medications for a year before she could apply for a good job? Where is the justice for that man who dutifully worked at a dead-end job for decades because he thought he was not smart enough to do what he loved, who stopped exercising his long-suppressed talent for art or math or organization or inventing bizarre and wonderful machines?

All forms of religious fundamentalism are based on the substitution of dogma for a living, complex, organic, common-sense reality. We are all born immersed in our own lived experience until it becomes corrupted by pressures to conform to somebody else's. Instead of responding with love, confusion, sympathy, and curiosity to a child who haltingly tells their parent that they are living in the wrong gender, we are told we must abandon empathy and impose a preordained label on the youngster. Instead of reaching with compassionate inquiry across lines of race and gender to stand in the reality of others and invite them into our own, we rely on stereotypes, assumptions, biases, and defensive refusals to listen born of guilt and misguided certainty. Not only do we accept a caricature of the other person's humanity, but we also grow ever more convinced that our version of that person's reality is the true one. Our understanding becomes increasingly distorted as we cling to it more and more vehemently.

Into this frozen silence between people of differing identities, we insert programs to promote diversity, equity, and inclusion—and we wonder why they fail.

Grim as this reality may be, there is another side to it: we also resist and reclaim rights and capacities. Even while Eladio internalized messages about his limitations, he engaged educational opportunities with pleasure and skill. Some of the ways we fight back mire us even more deeply in oppression, but still we carve out areas of control and authenticity. In all of the particular institutions that form the structure of inequality—some of which I'll explore in the following chapters—we also need to remember that there are living humans populating them, replete with contradictions: we submit and we resist, all in a moment. Even as we are divided, in some part of our being we may mourn the losses and maintain a capacity to unite, as we look to those who have broken through. Framing these contradictory forms of oppression and resistance are day-to-day engagements with social institutions: schools, workplaces, medical facilities, and so on. Each encounter contains messages about individual standing, rights, and restrictions as each impacts people of different social categories differently. In the two chapters that follow, I focus especially on how those dynamics play out in a context of racial discrimination. In the last chapter of this section, class becomes the framing concept, interspliced with other social identities, especially race and gender.

Part II
Institutions and Dehumanization

Why, man, he doth bestride the narrow world
Like a Colossus, and we petty men
Walk under his huge legs and peep about
To find ourselves dishonorable graves.
Men at some time are masters of their fates.
The fault, dear Brutus, is not in our stars,
But in ourselves, that we are underlings.

(William Shakespeare, Julius Caesar, Act I, Scene II)

…disability under capitalism is not just impairment—it is the lived experience of being positioned against the grain of a world calibrated for speed, profit, and extraction . . . . The "weight" one feels—the exhaustion of navigating inaccessible systems, the dread of a medical bill—is the superstructure pressing down like an iron sky.

Beatrice Adler-Bolton, "An Iron Sky Pressing Down: The Phenomenology and Political Economy of Expected Impairments." in "Blind Archive," Substack

9 **Religion**
And Its Mystifications

If we are to understand how we lost humanity, the concept of internalized oppression is key. Institutions order and shape the social world. Families, schools, churches, worksites, hospitals, government regulations, and revenue collection all organize time, daily activities, the architectural structures we live in, and the roads we travel. Beyond the physicality of these institutional manifestations are the ways they also shape our psyches. We've seen how they create limitations to the ways we think and the thoughts we share. We internalize ways to relate to others competitively or collaboratively and standards by which we judge ourselves and others.

Earlier, I suggested three ways we form knowledge of ourselves and the world: lived experience, interaction with people we encounter, and things we read or hear or see in impersonal media sources. These forms of interaction with our environments are the means by which we internalize culturally determinative messages. The particular messages we learn, and then so deeply normalize that we come to see as eternal truths, reflect the demands and needs of the societies we occupy. Different cultures, based in particular sorts of daily activities, rely differently on those three sources. Many of the villagers I came to know in Bangladesh had little access to media. News did make its way to them by hearsay, passed along often through many different people and heavily edited by what most interested those listeners and speakers. By the time news reached a particular person in the village, it had become a fine-grained amalgam of facts about events distant from them and gossip. But the particular gossip was not accidental either; news that a Muslim-dominated government had supplanted British rule was meaningful to both Hindus and Muslims in Panipur, translated through their own lenses into an opportunity for transforming power relations in everyday relations as well as the distribution of resources in the village where they lived, farmed, and fished. What was important was not so much what was happening in a distant capital but rather how people face-to-face talked about it, understood it, and therefore acted on it.

Dynamics in advanced capitalist societies in contrast privilege institutional knowledge over lived experience. We lose capacity for empathy in part because we are so often told that what our senses tell us is wrong. If it can't be proved, then it's unreliable. We do continue to talk with meaningful individuals and to be influenced by our "bubbles." But even more, we are shaped by the institutions with which we interact. In this part of the book, I look at several of those institutions to trace out how we become alienated from each other, detached from compassion, and led away from a morality of commonality into one of competitive difference.

Religion is a prime arena where a contradiction between human goodness and institutional constrictions plays out. That is not to deny how genuinely some people derive core spiritual sustenance from their religious practices. Many of the people I most respect are deeply religious, some through commitment to a particular church, others in more eclectic forms. Long ago, I rejected formal religious practice; I'll elaborate on the reasons later in this chapter. Spirituality, too, is troubling to me, in this respect: I regularly encounter people who believe it is possible to heal the world through spiritual means, and I am critical when I notice their absence from more in-the-world confrontations with oppression. Not that the two modalities are mutually exclusive: religiously motivated activists are a good example of both-and.

Where my personal convictions coincide with what I understand by "spirituality" is some amalgam of humanism and physics. We are all both matter and energy, specks in time and space, and inseparable from our human counterparts as part of the mass of creatures currently dominating the planet. My core commitment as an activist and a writer (a primary form of activism for me) is motivated by that belief in connectedness, whether we recognize it or not. Connection was not something I experienced in synagogue, however, a place where I felt my unconventionality to be highly unwelcome—although as I write that bitter sentence, I immediately think of the exception: the more orthodox rabbi in our community who welcomed my challenges and insistence on critical conversations about everything from morality to theology and politics: an age-old Talmudic tradition. Our long, loving, playful conversations did help to cheer me through some rough moments of adolescence.

This chapter is a political critique of religious institutions and their impact on society at large, non-believers as well as the faithful. However you worship, whatever form your spirituality takes, I invite you to accompany me as we make our way through important contradictions and complexities.

The Marriage of Religion and Politics

I write at a time when American polity has just taken an overt turn severely to the right. Less obviously, the moment in 2024 when Donald Trump was re-elected to the presidency was the culmination of years of planning and organizational work in the name of Christian autocracy, the seeding of a theologically grounded state.

Religion is a compound phenomenon. In fact, if we were to sum up all the elements I've written about so far in one equation—identity, worldview, professionalized solace, and categorical thinking—the result might be religion. At its best, religion offers people a collective identity that is rooted deep in childhood, family, community, and meaning. It frames a worldview, expressing a relationship between quotidian life and larger questions of the universe and spirit. Houses of worship are one of the few places in modern life where people can experience moments of quiet, a time when someone else is in charge and offers rituals that enable contemplation. This deep access to things beyond responsibility and aloneness, structured in companionship with others, briefly opens a door to connection ordinarily inaccessible in the rush of alienated lives. With connection comes comfort, a short respite from monkey mind (that constant judgmental self-talk that is the voice of internalized oppression) akin to the relief people may seek in psychotherapy.

Given all those benefits, it is surprising that so few people actually go to church. A recent Gallup poll in the United States revealed that only one in five Americans attends services weekly, and that number is declining.[1] In the UK, a study in 2025 surprised researchers by showing a growth in church attendance, especially among young men. Even so, only one in eight reported regular church attendance, the majority forsaking the Church of England for Roman Catholicism.[2] Even these low numbers of the weekly faithful have an impact, however. The influence of religious thinking goes far beyond the physical church.

Most religions impose strict rules of behavior, implanted as internalized ideology in the form of moral codes and instituting another form of alienation, in this case from one's lived, empathic sense of right and wrong. Little wonder then that churches are vulnerable to politicization. Many religious institutions offer ripe potential for organizing people based on definable principles of thought and behavior. Some churches use that capability for social good, integrating community service and progressive education into their practices. The Society of Friends (Quakers) is a prime example and the place where I first found a home for political activism. So also Baha'i with its grounding in the oneness of humanity, Unitarian Universalists, and progressive Jewish congregations and mosques, to mention a few, make valuable contributions to contesting problems of injustice.

Often, though, even the most conscious of religious institutions find themselves tangled in dynamics they have difficulty overcoming—the same dynamics common in secular organizations as well. I've been asked to help one progressive Christian congregation, for instance, work through conflict after assigning a charismatic Black man to take the pulpit of an older, all-white church with a dwindling congregation, in an attempt to revitalize it. Instead, he found himself thwarted by deeply unconscious forms of racism in his flock, well-meaning people with zero experience of multicultural relationships, no skill in sharing them, and deep resistance to engaging new ways of doing things. Other church-based groups sought mediation of conflicts involving convoluted problems of power sharing. A will to cooperate does not necessarily translate into the skills necessary to actually practice it. Whatever their theology and social orientation, religious institutions are still institutions, most commonly hierarchical organizations committed to unquestionable principles and as mired in culturally dominant ways of doing things as the rest of white society.

Contradictions and harms that derive from dogma are most vividly experienced by LGBTQ people. My practice and my world are filled with gay lapsed Catholics who spend a lifetime working to overcome wounds of homophobia inflicted by a church they once loved. Even as more congregations have declared themselves "welcoming," often biases toward normative family culture and heterosexual ethics alienate gay and lesbian congregants who may fall away from church attendance, worn out by struggling to overcome unawareness of majority members of the community. Trans people and others with non-binary gender identities give up insisting that people use requested pronouns. In the most traditional of churches, strict rules of morality are expressed in patriarchal control of basic, natural human wants, needs, and impulses. This war between empathic construction of behavior and tightly legislated rules plays out in many places, within institutional walls, inside human beings, and in the body politic, and especially on the souls of gay folks.

Religion's Role Supporting Authoritarianism

Authoritarian regimes commonly rest on religion. Hitler's extreme persecution of Jews contrasted with his reconstruction of Christianity in Germany under the control of the Nazi state. Religious identity laid a bold and broad border between those worthy of humanity and those destined for destruction. So also, fundamentalism in Muslim lands contrasts sharply with a deep humanitarian strain within Islamic thought and history. There is nothing in the Koran that dictates stern sharia law; that is a human interpretation subject to debate. Judaism similarly can swing either way: orthodoxy takes on a persona of patriarchal authoritarianism while liberal Jews practice a very different interpretation of doctrines.

In today's America, claims of absolute presidential authority and rapid action to dismantle anything resembling a welfare state are not always obviously grounded in theocracy, but religiosity nonetheless plays a subliminal role in its culture. On one level, President Trump promotes his unique ability and right to rule in terms that evoke divinity without outright claiming it. After an assassination attempt during a rally, Trump announced, "I felt very safe, because I had God on my side." Announcing he accepted what he perceived as persecution from his enemies "so you won't have to," he associated himself with Jesuitical martyrdom. Increasingly, as he campaigned for the presidency in 2024, he emphasized the idea that he and he alone could save the nation, that he made sacrifices in the name of his followers, that he escaped death only by the will of a higher deity.

Standing shadowed behind these sly references to religiosity lay other overtly religious actors. For decades before Trump's ascendancy, Christian conservatives planned a campaign to redirect American democracy toward the principles they promoted. Dating from the 1970s and advanced by the Reagan presidency, religious leaders came together with an intention to create a biblically based society. Thinkers like Paul Weyrich (founder of the Heritage Foundation), R. J. Rushdoony (founder of Christian Reconstructionism), and a coalition of evangelicals leading huge congregations across the country laid the groundwork for a theocratic culture and state. Less known as public figures than Moral Majority creator Jerry Falwell or other political grandstanders, these and other theopolitical ideologues notched incremental victories, one after another over many years, preparing for the Trump phenomenon.[3]

Who Organizes Social Change?

It is not hard to understand the successes of the Christian nationalists. When village rioters in Bangladesh explained to me that the plants and cows over which they fought were symbols, they opened up an explanation for what otherwise appeared irrational behavior. What they made visible was not something that happened—the riot—but something that did not: the absence of political routes to gain the rights and material resources they lacked but that sparkled before them in the atmosphere of rapid and dramatic change on the level of governance. In that political void, the villagers politicized their religious identities, organizing combat along lines of Hindu-Muslim animosity rather than a more direct pursuit of resources.

In the United States too, change has been advancing at a rapid pace since the end of the post–Second World War reconstruction. For twenty years, corporate structures planted roots deep in the soil of capitalism as it advanced globally. A certain stability lay over America as Europe regained prosperity and the colonial lands fought for independence. For me, growing up in this post-war period, stability seemed stifling. It lay like a heavy blanket over needed reforms, like desegregation, women's rights, and more. "Conformity" was the cultural norm of the time. Conformity meant acceptance of an unacceptable status quo.

But none of that contradicted the reality of radical change occurring beyond the awareness of a middle class, white, defined-as-straight young woman. What I felt in my bones and all the directions I chose for myself—activism, a transgressive marriage, emigration to India, for instance—reflected social changes I couldn't articulate but were heating to a boil under the surface of calm. Capitalism in this period tantalized the white middle class with the American Dream. It was this promise I heard evoked by the Central High School alumnae I interviewed. Having chased the Dream starting out in life in the 1950s, thirty years later, now at the age of retirement, they knew the Dream had failed. Despite their confusion, resentment, and fatigue, the goals continued to hold for them. They wanted stability, security, dignity, a boost for their children in the social order, and some degree of leisure-time pleasure.

American society as constituted not only did not deliver on that promise; it seemed to be redirecting it to people of color. The unfairness of that perception primed the white middle class Arkansans to be open to a very different promise. While they mourned the loss of the community they'd known in their youth, they understood it was the Faustian bargain they'd made in return for corporate protection: job security in return for moving their families at the will of their bosses. Internal migration was a keynote of the 1950s. When my family moved in 1951 from New York to Fort Worth, Texas, one of the first things my non-practicing Jewish parents did was to join a Jewish congregation. Identity as Jewish anchored their quest for community. So also the Christian folks from Little Rock shopped for churches where they could find some remnant of the kinship they had left behind.

Close under the lid of conformity during the 1950s bubbled the radicalism of the 1960s. One part of the cultural manifestation of rebellion was anti-church. To reject the moral dogmas of religion became a central and necessary part of opposition to the Vietnam War as well as to justifications for restrictions on the independence of women and continuing racism. A movement representing the rights of people with disabilities burst forth as well. Expressions of rebellion in sexual terms most overtly challenged the hegemony of Christianity. Both free love, the liberation of female sexual desire, and defense of homosexuality flew stridently in the face of everything churches taught and relied on for control.

And in turn, these oppositions stimulated resistance in the form of a new Christian conservatism, and right along with it Christian nationalism. With little alternative ideology formally organized, in the absence of a coherent political ideology and consistent political action to remake society as a collective of equals, there was nothing to compete with the intentional, unified efforts of the Christian right. Some voters vested hope in the Democratic Party which relied on promises of liberal reform; many lapsed as they witnessed promised progress rarely enacted and often undermined in practice. In a two-party electoral structure, some of us joked that our choices were between Tweedle Dee and Tweedle Dum. In truth, both parties remained captive to ever-increasing reliance on money and, at a deeper level, both dedicated whatever power they could access to the preservation of the same essential social order: patriarchal hierarchy.

Meanwhile, many different movements campaigned to address the real needs of different segments of the population: activism for racial equity, for feminist rights, for disability rights, and so on. But all these different objectives could not cohere into a whole and compelling program for the direction of society. Like so much else in the culture of capitalism, siloed in competing interests, they could not confront the greater context: that each was a manifestation of a social order incapable of meeting human needs because its objectives were vested in the accumulation of wealth, unfairly distributed, not in human well-being?

We live in a shared house with hard but crumbling walls, faulty plumbing, and unending rain soaking through the roof. My ultimate aim in writing this book is to engage in dialogue, learning ways to imagine and construct a new house, a sturdy and beautiful structure built on truth and equality. If that project has reality, it must challenge not only the ways we think about each other and the ways we treat each other—as essential as both those things are—but also the material realities that limit our access to the resources needed for shared well-being. We need not only to reclaim humanity but also to rebuild society to enable and encourage reconnection.

Let's go on to look at some other discomfiting rooms in our current house so we can begin that thoroughgoing redesign. In the next chapter, I focus on education systems and touch lightly on dynamics connected with housing and employment.

10 **Divide and Rule**
Education, Still Segregated After All These Years

In 1954, Thurgood Marshall achieved the major accomplishment of convincing the Supreme Court that separate but equal schools were not in reality even close to equal. Almost three-quarters of a century later, children of all complexions do share many schools. But in the first thirty years after *Brown v. Board of Education*, schools again grew more and more segregated by race, and that trajectory continues to this day.

There are several threads in this particular momentum of inequality. Almost as soon as schools actually integrated, city after city experienced something dubbed at the time "white flight." White families moved out of cities into suburbs where higher home prices both excluded families of color and simultaneously provided higher tax bases and therefore funding for schools. Inside cities, private schools grew up like weeds, reflecting the confluence of class and race: if you can't pay, you can't go. Many private schools nowadays do try in good faith to fund scholarships for students of color. But intention is not impact; often there are so few enrolled that kids find themselves suffering personal costs similar to those of the children who decades before were placed by ones or twos or nines in white schools to desegregate them. Private education remains heavily weighted toward a white population, while public schools in many cities have become majority Black and Brown.

In the 1980s demands arose for "school choice." Fueled primarily by conservative white parents, the charter school movement represented the underbelly of forced desegregation. For all the virtues of a neighborhood school system—attendance close to home builds community, encourages independence in children, involves parents more in school matters—if neighborhoods are divided by class, then schools remain segregated. The practice of busing kids to distant schools to mix populations made sense on paper but not in practice. Militant protests by white parents arose in cities like Boston, eventually developing into a movement for "school choice."

By deflecting resources from public to private schools, this charter school movement has had a measurable impact on re-segregating school systems. Across the country, racial segregation increased from the late 1980s until today in urban areas. According to researchers at Stanford University and the University of Southern California, districts where charter options were made available experienced the greatest increases, indicating that the choices a majority of parents made were for more racially separate schools. It may be that parents of color opted for situations offering particular protection and advantages for their children as well; remember Marian's comparison in an earlier chapter of how her older children prospered in segregated schools where teachers were more highly educated and distinctly more attentive to students who shared their identity, as compared to the neglect and alienation her younger kids experienced after school desegregation. Without question, most of the growth in predominantly white charter and private schools resulted from white parents choosing to take their children out of multiracial environments, either through school choice or by moving to majority white neighborhoods.[1]

In a sense, public schools are a laboratory for reflecting—and often, under-resourced and alone, to deal with—dynamics that sustain inequality in the greater society. Integrated schools are not intrinsically better for children, especially for kids of color. In fact, I've cited some evidence that teachers do a better job with students who share identity with them. Bias is hard to erase. This phenomenon of the resegregation of schools, however, exemplifies a dynamic of sustained inequality at a level hard to detect and therefore close to impossible to erase. Most parents choose schools for their children not based on racial demography but on accessing what they believe to be the best education for their kids.

Colluding with Injustice While "Minding My Own Business"

I made that choice. From the start of my son's school attendance, I was deeply committed to public education. I attended school board meetings and exercised every ounce of authority I could find to influence policies. I volunteered in the school, not just at PTA meetings but in the classroom. In fifth grade, my son attended a community school in San Francisco. When it was founded, a vibrant experiment in teacher-parent collaboration long before charter schools existed, the school was administered by committee and was known for innovative child-centered pedagogy. We occupied a large building in a bay-side part of the city. But there was a constant battle for resources. By the time my family entered the picture, we found many of the teachers to be exhausted by scarcity and conflict with the central school administration. At that time in my life, I was a dedicated artist, working figuratively in clay. I needed a studio; the school needed an art program. We made a deal. I set up a clay room in return for certain stated times I would be available to work with different groups of kids. What evolved, however, is that our tired, beleaguered teachers frequently sent children who disrupted their classrooms to me. I was also at the time learning to be a counselor and mediator in the alternative mode of Radical Therapy. The clay room became a de facto counseling center, the only counseling available in the building. I loved it, and so did the kids.

Teachers needed my resource in part because other schools in the system had taken to transferring their problem students to Community School. Many of these children were African American. As I got to know them, these frequent visitors to my clay room, I learned in detail how deeply they were misunderstood by well-meaning adults in the prior schools. In my long conversations with Tanya, for example, I was constantly impressed by her innovative cast of mind, equaled by her determination to create. We sculpted portraits of each other; I sent her home with a piece that I count among my best, and I treasure her vision of me. Antonio, on the other hand, started out wreaking havoc in the clay room, throwing clay around willy-nilly and impervious to my attempts to connect with him. Once I hit on the idea of his sculpting little warriors, complete with spears and swords that could be destroyed in battle with other little clay warriors, we had a much better time. That I was a volunteer served us well. "I don't have to be here," I'd say. "Make if fun for me and I'll make it fun for you." This mutuality was the key to our rich relationships.

But by the time my son was in seventh grade, the group of boys in his class were truly out of control. Most of the girls had transferred either to other classes or, when that wasn't possible, to other schools. The gender imbalance contributed to a problematic classroom dynamic beyond help even from the clay room. The teacher, an older, very kind white woman, eventually departed, literally hospitalized for psychiatric care. Frantic, our head teacher-committee implored the school district to provide a new teacher. It was near the end of the school year, so they offered substitutes who, one after another, quit after a day with this unruly group. Finally, as a serious recruitment effort for a new teacher got underway, I offered to step in until someone could be hired. We did okay, largely because I made no effort to enforce the required curriculum. Creative writing saved the day, along with lots of recess. I allowed sex as a topic.

Eventually relieved of classroom duty, knowing that my son faced another year with this particular mix of children and now with a newly hired teacher who applied military strategies with a heavy, anti-progressive hand, I made the hard decision to skip my boy into a private high school. Welcoming a child of color, so rare in their student body, and someone with a straight-A academic record, they awarded us a hefty scholarship. My father picked up the rest of the tab, support that accorded us a financial privilege I didn't myself have. So Tuhin received the most wonderful high school education imaginable. Not that there weren't problems and contradictions. The very first day he was there, in an orientation session with the headmaster, Tuhin mounted the first of recurring protests. The headmaster warned his white, middle-class charges to be wary of risks in the neighborhood. Tuhin stood up and said, "Hey, that's my neighborhood you're talking about! It's a perfectly fine neighborhood!" "Risk," he understood, was a euphemism for multiracial.

Racism, and many other forms of discrimination, happen not with intention but as incidental to other things. If Community School had been adequately funded, if all those other schools that dumped their "problem kids" to Community School had resources, if all those boys of color who were seen as problem kids had been recognized for who they were and treated with respect, dignity, and affection, we'd have stayed in the public school domain. We all focus on what beleaguers us and what we can control. And even as we focus there, we overlook the consequences in colluding with exclusion and injustice. Tanya and Antonio deserved an education as excellent as the one my son got.

Compounding Consequences

If all schools shared resources equally, as they do in Finland, there might still be other problems, but not the ones that bedeviled the segregated schools of Jim Crow America. That Marshall believed in the necessity of desegregation suggests an assumption that resources would never be equalized until white children attended every school: that is, all schools were integrated. In Little Rock, one of the many sources of resentment among the white alumnae I interviewed was that Central High—*their* school—was the one chosen to integrate. Central was the more working-class school. A new school recently opened in an affluent suburb remained all white, the old school in the African American area all Black.

After over seventy years of the experiment, we know that forced integration has resulted in people, young and adult, occupying the same buildings but failing to make genuine relationships or enjoy genuine equality. I recounted my story of Central High earlier: integrated by gross numbers, segregated by reality. The dynamics I saw there—Black kids in "regular" classrooms, white kids across the corridor in advanced placement classes—still far too commonly characterize public schools across the country. So many factors result in significantly more white students judged "qualified" for advanced placement curricula than students of color, starting with the question of who creates the qualifications. I see answers to this crucial question as spirals inside spirals. Let's start with the definition of "qualified."

Every culture designates certain ways of thinking as legitimate and others somewhere on a spectrum from tolerable to interesting to altogether bizarre and unacceptable. Where the current culture of the United States lands on that spectrum, and to a greater or lesser extent all developed capitalist societies, is very far toward legitimizing scientific rather than relational or creative thinking, a propellant of inequality I've addressed in an earlier chapter. That means that those trained to construct sentences in the form of subject-verb-object are given more credibility than those who start with dependent clauses, wander through imaginings, and land somewhere on an object with maybe a verb only implied. My friend SY often communicates with insightful questions rather than declarative sentences. Think of the lyrics to popular songs or the most lyrical forms of poetry. Rappers, for example, know well the power of unpredictability. In contrast, science builds each thought on the ones that came before. That is the way children in the dominant white culture are taught to talk and to think. When they get to the age of scholastic testing, therefore, they do better than kids raised on a more contextual, poetic, circular way of talking and thinking.

Many different institutional systems contribute to a race and gender-based discrepancy in access to what is normatively considered "success." More affluent parents who work only one job to support their families have more time to read to small children at bedtime. Quiet neighborhoods lend an environment in which studying may be more appealing to both kids and adults. Habits of thought and activity pass from generation to generation, increasing the odds that kids who live in more disorganized environments fit less well into the regimented routines they encounter at school and later in the workplace. Most schools teach writing as a template: you start with a topic paragraph, go on to elaborate your theme, and so on, ending with a conclusion. Some of the most eloquent papers I read when I taught at the college level started with a wish, a story, an imaginary conversation, then wandered through an elaboration. I fell in love with my spouse of more than thirty years when I read a paper she wrote in graduate school. Her assignment was something about how social workers should address a certain type of problem. Unable to connect with the topic, she escaped to the movies instead and saw "Thelma and Louise." Afterward, she finally forced herself to write and, still compelled by images from the movie, started her paper with a discussion of the film. In lyrical and discursive loops, she wove together various themes. Only at the very end did she bring it all home to answer the assigned question: brilliantly, I thought, connecting everything that came before but from a perspective she might never have articulated if not having journeyed through the themes and byways of the film. Her professor, less appreciative than I, marked her down for lateness and because he couldn't quite see that she had actually done what he assigned.

Many of my students at UC Berkeley, no matter what their identity, even though judged top students in their high schools as evidenced by their admission to this top-tier college, nonetheless couldn't string two sentences together in an easily understandable way. But even while I mourned how education had distorted the bell-clear, creative child voices I imagined they had lost along their way to higher education, I always made allowances for my students' bad writing. After all, my subject was conflict studies, not literature. If I could make sense of what they meant to say, I let it go.

One day, however, at the very end of the semester, the only time I assigned any writing longer than brief journal entries, I received a paper I truly couldn't understand, however many times I read it. I knew the writer to be a transfer student from a community college—many of my best students were in this category. Usually a bit older, having lived more complex lives, they brought to class their personal stories, lending depth to the very experiential classroom I ran. This student, a young African American woman, had been noteworthy in class. She participated freely in discussions, talked about her own spells of conflict, engaged in group activities with good spirit and enthusiastic leadership. But the paper she submitted was indecipherable, at least by me. I was pressed with end-of-semester paper marking and other bureaucratic business. I knew I would be justified to simply mark her down—she would pass anyway based on her classroom performances. Instead, I sent her an email asking her to come see me.

"What happened?" I asked, after explaining my difficulty reading her paper.

"Well, I did what you assigned, I thought."

"Maybe you did, but I can't get it from the way you wrote it. You speak so well; I would hate for whoever reads your writing to miss out on what you have to say because it's not clear. Do you know that there's a writing clinic on campus? Would you consider getting support from them?"

"I did that," she declared in a voice crackling with annoyance. "I wrote this paper using the outline they gave me. I thought I wrote it exactly the way they told me to."

We both sat and puzzled. So I invited her to speak what she meant to write to me. She ran out a thoughtful and thorough response to the question I'd posed in the assignment. As she spoke, her voice grew stronger, her expression more and more filled with energetic asides and illustrations. I listened, rapt.

"Brilliant!" I exclaimed when she'd finished. "Do you have time to go home and write what you just said, exactly how you said it, while you still remember?"

Her eyes slaked sideways. "If I go home, my daughter will be there with my grandmother; she's three and very clingy to me right now. The dishes will still be in the sink, the laundry will be staring at me wanting to be folded. If I go home, I certainly won't write it!"

"Sit here." I stood up, offering my chair and my laptop. "I'll leave you for a little while. Write, and leave it on the computer for me to read when I come back."

Later, I found one of the most compelling student papers ever gifted to me.

We've seen the consequences of this phenomenon again and again as we seek to understand why professions (in my case, specifically mediation and ADR or Alternative Dispute Resolution, the term most common in legal circles) are dominated by people of dominant identity. When colleagues and I launched an organization (Practitioners Research and Scholarship Institute or PRASI) intended to sponsor writers of color to use their experience as research and to write, we quickly discovered one aspect of the imbalance: the numbers of talented practitioners of color who are ABD: "all but dissertation." "I just couldn't write the way they wanted me to," people exclaimed. "I don't think that way." Again and again, we saw people struggle to produce draft write-ups of their culminating research only to have "advisors" (actually judges) turn them back for re-draft. How many bright minds and capable practitioners have been lost to law, medicine, and other fields because of this serious disjunction between legitimized ways of thinking, speaking, and writing that hold the keys to practicing in professions? How many people never even get that far but drop out, often feeling inadequate, before the end?

We could layer this particular barrier with many others: the cost of higher education; the failure of mentoring for students, especially students accustomed to being marginalized elsewhere; the alienation of campuses where so few people "look like me." When my student talked in class about her lived examples of conflict, often her stories were about things that had happened in classes at Berkeley. Of course, she had plenty of other examples from many, many parts of her life. My class tended to draw students of color, especially athletes who often found a lone source of funding for advanced studies in sports; I tried to craft my curriculum to accommodate their stressed schedules and complicated lives. But also, they told me, they enrolled in my class because it was the only place they'd found on campus where they could talk openly about their painful experiences of racism. To sit in classes day after day, silent and hurt and angry, deeply alienated, is not a recipe encouraging the perseverance necessary to advance.

Time Oppression

Before I move on to other institutional factors that keep society segregated, white people unaware, and people of color disadvantaged, I want to mention one that laces through it all: time. Time is an artifact of culture. How we account it, organize it, value it, impose it: all the many ways time structures our lives reflect history and social position. All that has always been true; agricultural societies structure time around the sun and the seasons; industrialized ones obey the needs of the assembly line and the time clock. Some of my Black friends make jokes about "CPT": "colored people's time." It's a very familiar dynamic among us: I'm always promptly on time for our get-togethers, they're frequently late. Actually, what that means is, late by my clock, not theirs. If they were meeting other Black friends who understood time as they did, they'd be just on time. Time in India is judged by a different clock than time in Singapore, time in Italy differently than in Germany. To inhabit an Italian sense of time while living in Germany spells trouble. So too for many Americans of color who daily must adapt to an American industrial clock.

If production is done by craft workers in home settings with the participation of family members, then work fits around human needs as well as the needs of the market. Once production moves to a collectivized factory, once its pace is set not by human capacity but by demands of profit-making and marketing patterns, then humans are forced to comply with *those* needs, not their own. Many people confronted the clash between these two systems of time accounting during the Covid-19 pandemic when so many of us worked from home. The timing of a two-year-old didn't meld well with the demands of the Zoom clock.

My friend and colleague Roberto Chené has dubbed this ubiquitous dynamic "time oppression." The structure of most schools enforces obedience to this harsh clock. Every parent of school-age children knows how hard it is to get kids to conform to an institutional schedule. Early mornings are prime time for family conflict. Classes start too early to accommodate children's biological needs for sleep, not to mention their needs for play, exploration, discovery, and just tuning out. How many parents command kids to dress, only to find them many minutes later sitting on the floor delighted with a new monster they've just created from Legos? Much research has shown that early morning starting time for classes is especially oppressive for teenagers.

Once in the school building, kids must conform to set curricula taught for specified periods of time. For a too-brief two years in fourth and fifth grades, I attended a one-room school taught by a super gifted teacher named Bill Hickey. I loved math; Bill allowed me as much time as I wanted to play with arithmetic and, later, equations. He set long pieces of butcher paper across the floor and threw math challenges at me all day while he tutored other kids in multiple subjects, and I worked out the answers at my pace and pleasure. Little wonder that I loved school and that I graduated college with a major in math. Along the way, we all also prospered in English, sciences, and other subjects, taught with similar attention to who each of us was.

For those children in our polyglot society who carry cultural sensibilities of time more flexibly than dictated by the majority, tardiness and truancy occur at measurably higher rates. In the 2022–23 school year, American Indian and Pacific Islanders had the highest absentee rates in American schools, followed closely by Black children. Difficulties getting to school, of course, derive not only from culture but also from the many other institutional impediments I've mentioned, connected with class and the physical arrangement of our cities and towns that impede easy access by young people and over-busy adults.

Fitting the Child to the System or Vice Versa: The Finnish Miracle

Once at school, all kids suffer from the industrialized world's insistence on filling every minute with "productive work." Finland realized this problem and famously made increased recess time a priority, as well as making other changes to accommodate the way kids actually prosper rather than struggling to shape them to ways they don't. It turned out that their system produces impressive academic results as well as happier people. When every three years the Program for International Student Assessment (PISA) tests fifteen-year-olds in eighty-one countries, students in Finland consistently score at the top end, unlike those in the United States somewhere in the middle. The differential is not accidental; many intentional policies create Finland's greater success, starting with when children start school: at age seven instead of five as in the United States. Before then, they may go to pre-school where their day is filled with creative play but where instruction is strictly outlawed.

One of the well-noted problems of American education is that girls are neurologically ready for the sedentary work of academic learning, especially reading, sooner than boys. Fidgety youngsters not only don't learn skills but also internalize messages that they are bad or rowdy when frequently chastised. They may also conclude that they're simply not good at scholarship or, like the boy I interviewed in Little Rock, not smart, or like the boys in Allentown, troublemakers, or like the boys I taught in San Francisco, recalcitrant rebels determined to wreck the system. Recognizing the importance of free play and physical movement, the Finnish government mandates that schools give kids at least fifteen minutes of play for every forty-five minutes of learning; most American school children get somewhere around half an hour during a longer school day. The school day in Finland begins later and ends earlier than in the United States. Everything about the Finnish school system is cast in terms of evening out social inequality; every school is public, receives equal government funding, and is staffed by teachers with master's degrees earned with support from state grants. Teacher salaries are kept comparable to those of doctors and others with high social status.

Finland proves that public policies can make a difference. In the United States, however, conventional policies seem tilted toward producing graduates who consent to conditions that perpetuate existing discrimination and inequality. To ensure public funding sources, governments require metrics which translate into teaching to testing that interferes with teachers' ability to focus on relationships should they have a will to do that. Underfunding overpacks classrooms so that even those teachers who want more to tailor teaching to learning needs lack the time and support needed. Structure and policy constrict imagination and empathy within school parameters, step by step confining expansive child energy into socially legislated adult consent.

Now imagine what happens when these children grow up and enter the workforce. Saturated with competitive judgment, unschooled in building cooperative relationships, accustomed to working in isolation, people find themselves in daily settings where the things they do must be integrated into the activities of many coworkers. Not surprising, then, that workplaces are a prime market for conflict resolution "professionals." So many of the fault lines develop along fault lines of identity that Equal Employment Opportunity mediators, human resources managers, and company ombudspersons are in frequent demand.

11 **Multicultural Workplaces**
Conflicts Both Interpersonal and Systemic

I've focused on education systems because they are the earliest encounter with institutional life for most children and therefore a primary location for internalizing social hierarchy and categorization: who is black, brown, white, or purple, and which is better or worse? But the impacts of many other systems collude with and continue that alienating process. We could look, for example, at the problem of housing, a place where kids experience segregation even before school. Neighborhoods are almost as segregated as they were in the time of southern Jim Crow, before legislation outlawed housing discrimination but failed to prevent it. Where back then, however, Black, Latino, or Asian majority neighborhoods were genuine communities of care, now segregated housing accords few protections and many risks. Highly associated with economic disparities, including how very profitable real estate markets create scarcity and inflated costs of living, segregated neighborhoods inevitably reflect class. Dynamics of crime, chaos, noise, and lack of access to sources of nutritious food all show up as problems of the schools as well.

So many forms of inequality intersect, and each has been researched and reported in many places. I'm thinking of the medical system, for instance. Access to healthcare is uniquely challenged in the United States. We look with envy at universal providers in Canada, Cuba, the EU, and so many other places. Instead of advancing toward emulating these single-payer systems, having made timid advances in the Obama administration, America now marches backward. Even the meager supports of federal systems like Medicaid are currently being deprived of funding, stranding millions of struggling people without access to the doctors and medicines on which they depend.

For all the interlocking institutional systems we might explore that contribute to dehumanizing populations, I want to focus on what comes after school: the job market. American education highly privileges academics and slights practical training. Apprenticeship is left to labor organizations, which themselves have declined in numbers, reach, and effectiveness since the 1980s when President Ronald Reagan began a sustained attack on them. Workers' advocacy has grown far worse ever since, compounding the constriction of protected jobs available to people without college degrees. All these trends in the nature of work contribute to the expanding chasm between haves and have-nots.

Meeting and Conflicting on the Job

The workplace is the one place where people of different identities do come together. But often the conditions of their meeting exacerbate conflict rather than promoting amity. I'm thinking of all the mediations I've been asked to do because of "personality conflicts" between coworkers. Often, "personality" turns out to be a code word for race or sexuality. Employees of different races and backgrounds cast together without facilitation very often hit minefields of cultural difference, and even more, of deeply embedded inequality. On further exploration, we soon discover that whatever incompatibilities exist on an interpersonal level are playing out in an organizational framework that sets people up to be at odds with each other. Job descriptions are vague, lines of authority confused, management ill-equipped, and "teamwork" mystified by hidden realities of hierarchy.

Just as the authorities in Little Rock failed to provide students at Central High with guidance about how to create an inclusive community, similarly little or no support—at least, no effective support; the next chapter critiques DEI programs—tends to be available to employees required to work together. Some wise person asked, did we do all this to bring about integration only to sit in a room and not know how to have a conversation? Worse yet, when relationships are forced across different cultures and communities, they tend to become toxic. Remember how Adi explored his differences with Shelby in Chapter 2? He used all his senses: his recognition of how each of them lived, his intuition about Shelby's sadness, his creative ability to link the two perceptions, and his ability to ask questions and get answers. That's what's missing at work. People may perceive a coworker's approach to a task as different from their own and draw distorted conclusions: "Gee, I'd pull the file first and set up time with the legal department only after I've thoroughly understood what's in it. Why is this new staff person already on the phone asking for legal consultation?" Perhaps in childhood the onlooker had been chastised for asking questions. "Figure it out yourself," whether overtly spoken or covertly urged by adult inattentiveness to kids' curiosity, is one of those injunctions that reinforces individualism. Perhaps having internalized this individualist order and stopped asking for help, they now feel competitive with the newcomer who goes straight to the authority, seesawing between one-down jealousy and one-up moral superiority. Not surprising then when they turn these painful judgments on this unknowing coworker. All that secret, internal struggle is exhausting. Before anything has really happened, this worker is primed to mistrust and resent their new colleague.

Fantasizing Cooperative Processes

Compare that imagined scenario—hypothetical but not at all far from what I've encountered many times over the years as a mediator!—with this one. I mean what follows not to be a script but rather a musing: what if . . . ?

Newcomer: Hi! My name is NC. You're OT, yes? Our supervisor tells me I'm supposed to join your team to produce Project J.

Old timer[eyes glued to desk]: Oh, yes. I've been expecting you. Here's a print-out of all the tasks involved. Young coworker [YCW] at that desk over there is probably the best person to take on these items, and these others need my experience. So here's your list.

YCW[Leaping up, hand extended]: Hello there! I'm YCW; my pronouns are they them. And yours?

NC: Glad to meet you, YCW. I'm old-fashioned, still use she her. Are you new here? Did you go through orientation?

YCW: No, I'm sort of an intern, even though I think they have me doing a full-on job.

NC: Well, I propose we three have a chat about how we want to work together on the project. OT, are you up for that.

OT [grumpily]: Well, I'm kind of busy but I guess so. [picking up the list]

NC: Let's go get a cup of coffee.

Leaving the office may change the feeling of the conversation, humanizing it. People have to chat about something on the way to a café: Nice weather we're having, yes? Do you come to this café often? and so on people get a tiny bit of contextual information about each other, noticing what others order, how they treat the barista, where they choose to sit—simple things that are not obvious in a static office.

> YCW: You know, I've been thinking this project could be sort of fun, although I'm kind of dreading the tasks you've assigned me, OT.

> NC: They offered some suggestions in my orientation about how to start a team project, getting to know each other. If you're both game to try, I am. One of the first questions is, "How do you like to work in a group?"

> OT: What kind of question is that?! I like to figure out what needs to be done, what the timeline is, assign everyone certain tasks, and dig in. Is there any other way?

> NC [While YCW squirms, lips pulled tight]: Well, yes. I like to look at what we're asked to produce and brainstorm different ways to go about it. I don't know you well enough to suggest a little mind-opening smoke might be involved. But even without that, it can be fun to get imaginative and throw out all kinds of ideas about how to do this thing—even what this thing we're doing actually is and where it fits into a larger picture.

> YCW: [jumping in their seat]: Yes, yes! That sounds great. I like to take my time, play with different approaches, get on social media to get stories about how other people have done something similar, and gradually settle on how I want to do it. Unfortunately, that sometimes confuses me and often makes me late—looks a lot like procrastination because I never talk about what I'm doing with teammates. I know they'd disapprove [looking sidewise at OT who returns the glance not unsympathetically]

> NC: That suggests another question the orientation folks proposed: How do you get in trouble when working in a group? I know how I do: I don't pay much attention to a timeline, although I always have one eye on the deadline. Meanwhile, my coworkers get really antsy wanting me to stop talking about the process and just do it. I don't mean to stress them but somehow, I do. Is that happening already now?

> OT: [with a chuckle]: Not yet, although I can see the possibility in our future. But that's kind of a good question. Makes me realize how often I end up hating everyone and feeling like a martyr. I plunge in, direct

everyone else, notice that YCW isn't getting anything done and feel
very resentful when I remind him . . . uh, them . . . that time is wasting.
Meanwhile, I lose sleep doing it all myself, so even when others on
the team do produce their work, I've gone to the next step and need
to redo what they've done. None of it is fun! I'd way rather do it all
myself—and get paid more!

It would not be difficult in my scenario to color the characters with identities
based in race, gender, and generation. What if they wander conversationally
beyond their work relationships and begin talking about their cultures
and backgrounds? I can imagine stories emerging about how they were
raised, what they've experienced in other workplaces, how some of these
same dynamics get them in trouble at home, and so much more. As these
human relationships grow in depth and sympathy, they now become
capable of talking through their cultural differences insofar as they show up
in conflicting ways of thinking and working. What if they begin to fantasize
ways to make those differences work for them, inventing ways to keep the
conversation going so nobody is left guessing and together they can revise
as they go? All that takes time. What if they feel entitled and empowered
to go to their manager and explain what they need to do the project in a
way that works for them as well as for the organization? What if they were
encouraged to participate in the process of setting timing—or even to
question the usefulness and direction of the project itself? We're moving here
into the territory of shared management and decision making, imagining an
organization pledged to collective process rather than profit-driven hierarchy.
What if these liberated workers awarded themselves raises, dipping deeply
into the profits derived from their work and flowing to people never seen in
the office or on the factory floor?

Perhaps that's why conversations like the one I've imagined aren't built into
most organizational proceedings where profits do matter. Doing things
in a way that promotes well-being for the actual humans doing the work
threatens the expectations of the absent humans expecting to claim the
excess value produced by sped-up work, in the form of returns on investment
or profit. If we were to extend the fantasy of humane workplaces, we might
soon find ourselves considering well-resourced neighborhoods, curiosity-
focused schools, and so much more—revolutionary changes that serve all
people in ways that also keep open the empathic pathways so forcefully
slammed shut in our present systems. Empathy turns difference into a thing

of wonder, something to be engaged and explored and delighted in. We might find ourselves on a wave of revolutionary change—but that's getting ahead of my story.

Instead, employees sit daily witnessing others' actions without understanding them, and certainly without benefiting from differences they disrespect and fear. In situations of unfamiliarity, we all draw on everything we've experienced before to make as much sense of things as we can. When the unfamiliarity carries an intimation of unknown differences, when, in other words, our sense of danger is heightened, then we work double time to understand what the differences and dangers are, in order to better take care of ourselves. In work settings, if the newcomer is a person of color, or a woman in a male-dominated profession, or a transgender person who unsettles acquaintances' intuitive sense of social category, or a person with limited vision, or one of so many other characteristics that we find unusual, then the process of perception-intuition-explanation-conclusion all done internally, not a word spoken, is almost destined to go awry.

Seeing how alienated dynamics play out, resulting in dysfunctional operations and disruptive conflicts, some companies in past years turned to the process Donald Trump so decisively turned against: DEI training.

12 Diversity and Other Misnomers

What's the Matter with DEI?

When Donald Trump put DEI in the center of his bullseye, he had a point. Sometimes, what begins as a movement toward equity and justice bends and twists along its life path into something more contradictory. In a foundational sociology book called *Poor People's Movements*, Frances Fox Piven and Richard Cloward trace the ways dynamic, grassroots social protest movements become contained as they progress from upwellings of discontent into organizations. The momentum of capitalist dynamics mutes their transformative potential, enfolding it in corporate and entangling it in financial snares.

Diversity training was never itself a social movement. Instead, it was an outgrowth of methods for identifying and challenging white racism. There is value in tracking interpersonal transactions that enact racism in day-to-day life, using knowledge born from honest dialogue, however confrontational, to teach people how to alter behaviors. As more and more companies instituted diversity hiring practices, more and more conflict emerged. Nobody really knew how to bridge cultural differences, nor certainly to account for the wounds people brought into the workplace or the university from lifetimes of injurious racially based experiences. Human Resources staff, charged with managing these disruptions, called in professionals, and a whole new profession of "diversity specialists" arose, promising workshops and advice. Teaching lessons on unconscious bias, identifying microaggressions and other forms of disaffecting interaction, they sought to re-educate adults even as they were constrained from delving into deeply embedded divisions by terms of their contracts. Most established institutions want their personnel to "act better" but not to challenge fundamental ways of doing business.

But if disaffection between white people and others of color most often is grounded in organizational and systemic realities, in facts and factors integral to the organizations for which they work and by socioeconomic realities way beyond them, then teaching people how to talk to each other doesn't do more than brush honey over a bitter problem. People exercise their "bullshit meter" and end up cynical about new rules of comportment taught by a new brand of "experts." Adding to these rough feelings, workers are very aware that acting as directed is not voluntary; standing close behind the DEI trainer is a boss. Resentment smolders, often exacerbating bad feeling in the relationships meant to be improved.

The Fury of Trumpian Opposition to DEI

Nonetheless, it was not the inadequacy of programs seeking to rectify racism that prompted the second Trump administration to ban all mention of DEI. That these programs failed to make a substantial dent hardly accounts for such strenuous attempts to erase all awareness of racial or gender inequality from the American consciousness. Among a flurry of executive orders signed by Trump on the day of his inauguration was one ordering federal agencies and departments to cancel all programs intended to correct historic discrimination in education, hiring, and services. To me, the ferocity of the attack and its thoroughness reek of fear. What danger so challenged this man and his minions who claimed to themselves so much power that the very naming of diversity had to be prohibited?

The breadth of his list suggests an unsavory passion. Diversity, equity, and inclusion became forbidden words, the acronym DEI leading the charge. Along with those three words, commonly used to indicate programs and activities meant to correct long-standing wrongs, the president also banned whatever words identified the groups he meant to eclipse: "Black" was on the list, the color as well as the racial identity. So also were "Latinx." "Native American," "multicultural," even the word "race" itself. "Diversity" and all its derivations, whether "racial" or connected with "community," were ordered to disappear. The elimination of language with which to distinguish differences went well beyond race. "LGBTQ" and "transgender" did not surprise me—Trump had long made known his antipathy to anything encompassed by the broad term queer, although interestingly that word itself escaped censorship—but I was given pause by "woman." Those working for Washington were not to mention "female," "gender," or even that mainstay of the nation's capital, "sex." If people could no longer engage this category of difference, neither could they write the word "elderly" nor reference those requiring "accessibility."

Despite its inadequacies on the ground, work on anti-racism did produce certain results. We've learned so much about the day-to-day details of how racial wounding occurs. I know from my work as a mediator and as a teacher of young adults how powerful it is to listen attentively to the stories of people who have been discounted, demeaned, ignored, and overlooked, not once but again and again and again. Witnessing the anger and grief people express feels like an honor, especially because right along with it, in my experience, comes reciprocal kindness and laughter and, most importantly, connection. Listening can be difficult for white people; we tend to hear these stories as criticisms, laced with accusations of ill intent. One of the gifts of the DEI movement is the distinction between impact and intention. In another context, it might matter what I meant by what I said or did, or why I said it. But all that is very different from how it landed. The very first thing I learned in working across lines of race is this: if somebody tells me I did or said something that conveyed racism to them, they are right. It's my job to connect the dots, not with guilt, but with gratitude for a deepened understanding of how racism happens and how I participated. The premise is that my intention was not to do harm, but that I nonetheless have been induced to do exactly what I did not intend. How did that happen—to me? How was my moral course altered by my own socialization into whiteness?

It's not difficult to translate this process to sexism. Every woman knows how injurious, how infuriating it is, to tell a man you're angry because he took a tool out of your hand or overexplained something you already know or assumed the right to make certain decisions without consulting you. If once you've expressed your hurt and anger, the guy responds with an explanation—or worse yet, says, "Calm down. Why are you so upset? I didn't do anything," he's lucky if he escapes with his shins intact, as well as other parts of his anatomy. Translate these dynamics into some way you've been misunderstood, your dignity undermined, your reality questioned; every one of us has experienced some variation because we've all been young, required to sit quietly in a kindergarten classroom, bullied by an older child, or told not simply that we can't do what we want to do but that we're somehow wrong to want it.

Given that I, too, have been on the receiving end of dominance, when I hear that I've caused pain to someone else, it takes a good deal of self-prompting to remember that I am a good person. That is especially true if I'm totally mystified by what I've done and why it was painful to you. The temptation to excuse my actions, to defend myself against some imagined attack, to explain myself or to retaliate with counter accusations, is very strong. Procedural trainings in DEI too often touch the behavior surface of these transactions and reactions without providing the relationship-building that comes from elaborated storytelling and listening. The "good intentions" of the effort may drive deeper wedges between people who work together or sit in classrooms where truthful dialogue remains silenced. It is one more wedge, one more insult or "microaggression" added to all those created and maintained by the socioeconomic systems we inhabit.

Political Uses of Divided Populations

Much has been researched, written, and published about how these and other interlocking social systems, sustained by public policy decisions, create insurmountable obstacles to progress toward social equality. The particular thread in that weave I mean to draw out here is how the barriers simultaneously exist "out there" in the institutional terrain and "in here," in our identities, worldviews, and beliefs. What we think, how we think, what interferes even with access to concepts in which to think, all stem from the ways our most fundamental institutions are constructed. And those particular ways impact consciousness by fitting us to accept the unacceptable. Then, when we experience unacceptable personal distress or social failures, we do accept them, either seeing ourselves as defective (often defined in psychiatric terms) or blaming others (often in racial or class terms).

Both identity-based divisions and psychiatrized self-blame lend themselves to political manipulation. Colonial rulers long appreciated the gift of identity conflict as a lever for "divide and rule," and they fanned the flames in every way they could. The British Empire in India is the poster child for that process. Donald Trump plays chords of racism as an overt strategy for attaining power. We cannot know whether he truly believes what he says, but it doesn't really matter. Whatever the reality, those chords existed long before Trump's ascendancy, lying deep in the American experience.

As life goes on, the institutional separations I've sketched in the previous chapters increase instead of diminishing. Housing, for example, offers scant opportunities for mingling, remaining mostly segregated by class, which in the United States and most European nations coincides with race. Even where people may share neighborhoods or structures (I'm thinking of the many high-rise lofts and apartments in San Francisco or New York, London or Berlin), all the internalized rules of privacy interfere with building friendships or multiracial community, indeed, any community at all. Fundamental to drawing people close is truth: talking honestly about one's joys and sorrows, seeking support and counsel, showing up with food and recognition and affection. But neighbors who escape the hard walls of homes and apartments in order to engage in this way are rare, even when people share identity. Paradoxically, the walls grow harder where adversity is least. Need propels people into community, but if we think we should be secure and content because we are prototypically middle-class folks, then we stay home and don't recognize our need for support. Where differences of identity, especially race, factor in, prevailing alienation is compounded by multiple dynamics of bias.

School communities sometimes offer more opportunities for interaction. Parents may serve on committees where they encounter people different from themselves. Children's friendships sometimes stimulate connections among their family members. But even small children pick up messages that keep them separate. Even when family members, both juvenile and adult, wish to have more interaction with acquaintances from school, scarcity of time often interferes, as well as more complex dynamics having to do with internalized injunctions about parenting.

When I published a volume about conflict and cooperation in families, instead of a book tour I arranged a series of workshops on what I called "cooperative parenting." Some of these took place in co-housing projects. These excellent attempts at enabling community originated in Scandinavia and now exist in the United States, dotted across the continent. Their unique design gives people private units as well as access to common ones. Often, there are shared guest quarters, laundries, storerooms, and, most importantly for supporting true community, shared kitchens. The residents in these communities universally talked about their decision to move into the project because they craved a more peopled daily world, for their children and for themselves. They believed in sharing, wanted to show up for neighbors in need, and were thrilled at the easy access their kids had to other children and to a safe outdoor environment.

I had thought people in these communities would already be practicing much of what I preached in my book. Instead, I found that sharing stopped when parents experienced trouble parenting. "How do you all deal with the hard moments with your kids?" I asked. "I go to therapy," said one mom. "I read a book," said another. "I go to bed and hope it will pass," said a third.

Surprised that nobody described turning to a neighbor, I pressed them. "Have you ever asked another parent in the community for help? Why not?"

Silence as people looked sideways, trying, I thought, not to catch anybody's eye. Finally, one brave mom said, "I feel ashamed. I should know what I'm doing, and I don't."

Heads nodded around the room. Fear of being judged by others layered on top of judgments with which parents torment themselves, enforcing silence. Even in these intentional communities, places where people seek to escape the separating walls of private living to the greatest extent possible, these other intangible walls kept people separate when it came to the most painful of problems they experienced. No more were they sharing details of their financial problems, or what kept them separate from their partners in bed. Money, sex, and parenting are forbidden subjects in this culture, encrusted in judgment and shame.

So if proximity in schools and living environments are limited vehicles for constructing genuine cross-identity relationships, what about work? In the previous chapter, I sketched some of the reasons why here as well proximity does not necessarily breed familiarity, even though work is the place where more adults find themselves required to engage in meaningful processes with people from different backgrounds and heritages. My mediation practice is sustained by cross-cultural conflicts in these settings. That's no wonder. If everything that has come before has given people no experience of multicultural interaction, then little wonder that they come to the workplace ill-prepared even for the imagined explorations I suggested earlier. If in addition fear and shame cause them to look away from conflict rather than engaging it as a meaningful way to learn about others, then they are locked into a kind of alienation that smothers direct exploration and compounds prejudicial assumptions, fear, and, once again, that most relationally lethal of feelings, shame. Codes of silence are enforced and reinforced such that whatever changes of attitude might occur don't.

Most white people may not literally fear a stranger in the night wiping them out, but many do fear the reaction of people of color were they honestly to express what they think. And they are partly right: what they think may well *be* injurious. However well-intentioned—the justification we so often offer after realizing we caused pain—the impact on people of color of what we've expressed is hurt, and, yes, sometimes anger. When the person hurt feels so injured that they turn away from interaction, weary of explaining their reality to white people who in any case may not seem (or be) open to hearing it, the impasse remains frozen.

One aspect of the asymmetry characterizing race relations in America is that people consigned to the social margins know a great deal more about people in the center than the other way around. The culture offers up copious, elaborated, complex stories, images, films, and so on portraying white experience more generously than those representing the true reality of people of other identities. Even as Black, Asian, Native American, Latino, and other stories have found greater representation in recent decades, productions by people of those identities about their own experiences are rare. Funding flows to those movies and shows that promise to attract the largest audiences with the most money to spend on the products advertisers seek to sell. And so when people find themselves needing to understand each other in institutional settings like school and work, white people are often surprised by things their colleagues of color express, while the opposite is less rare. When people of color do decide to voice the pain they feel because of an ill-advised comment by a white person, they may well be met by disbelief, argument, defense, or any one of a number of other responses that suggest the reality must be otherwise. Acknowledgment of our reality is something we all fight for; marginalized people, experiencing instead frequent discounts of what they say happened, may well finally decide simply to keep quiet and, often, ultimately to leave. In an earlier chapter, I wrote about an exchange with an African American woman as we prepared for a mediation. "Do you feel alienated?" I asked. "Of course," she answered. "This is America."

Attrition rates in employment can be attributed in large part to this dynamic. People of a variety of identities may be recruited and hired, but repeated transactions that leave them feeling hurt, misunderstood, discounted, and demeaned hasten their departure for greener pastures—which, however, may be hard to find.

In all these ways, institutional dynamics of racism become fueled by internalizations of them and the frayed relationships that result. In turn, these widening breaches among people of different identities enable the institutional inequalities to persist. Why, despite Supreme Court orders, civil rights legislation, and massive public campaigning for equality, does racism persist? Is it any wonder?

Gendering Divisions

Before I leave this account of how systemic and interpersonal phenomena interact to lock in racial injustice, defeating past DEI programs and policies, I want to say a bit about how these dynamics work in terms of gender. People of differing races can manage to avoid each other to a greater or lesser extent, depending on circumstances. But heterosexual people (and many LGBTQ people as well) cannot. Racist estrangement can be locked out at the front door; but the groom carries gender struggle right along with the bride across the threshold.

Women of oppressed racial and cultural identities encounter many barriers and hardships that differ from white women's. The double jeopardy of race and gender is a vivid reality people face every day. At the same time, all women face a common class discrimination, its impact muted or heightened by race, disability, immigration status, age, and other factors but laced through it all. Women earn less for the same work; even more impactfully, most women work in professions that are consistently undervalued in most capitalist economies. By dint of particular talents and education, individual women may prosper more than their less advantaged sisters. But even in highly paid technological, scientific, and financial fields, complaints abound that women continue to be paid less, promoted less often, and supported less by their institutions when they find themselves in conflict.

I've written earlier a bit about how these dynamics manifest in screening women out of positions of power, both politically and in the economy. At home, they are compounded by the "second shift," in Arlie Hochschild's artful phrase.[1] Despite some loosening of a strict separation of gendered responsibilities, women still do a whole lot more domestic labor than their menfolk. One of the more progressive changes of the last twenty years is the recognition by men that their lives are enriched, and along with spousal amity, their sex lives improved, when they are more involved with their children on a day-to-day basis. I watch with heartfelt admiration when I see young fathers diapering, feeding, coddling, and comforting their young ones.

My own father was a warm-hearted man; as the town doctor he excelled at hands-on care for his patients. He played with us often, but he spent no time rearing us, never changed a diaper or, in my memory, fed us. He and I had a contentious relationship, despite (or maybe because of) a strong synergy between us. Late in life, I invited (or cajoled or demanded?) him to a let's-finally-work-it-out conversation. We went for a drive; I told him why I was so often so angry at him, and he told me some of the impact my disaffection had on him over the years. Recognizing each other's truths, we both apologized—and to my amazement my father wept. Only once before had I seen that happen, when the teenaged child of close family friends died. Now, as the tears slid down his cheeks, he said, "I never knew I could talk like this!"

Not every mother knows she can either, but the daily, constant closeness with her children, the detailed knowledge of the bodily habits of another human being, the need to protect and care even when exhausted and confused, all that living life in close proximity to other human beings opens the psyche to certain intuitive, hopefully empathic channels. Men who do not care for others, who do not have the opportunity of being face-to-face with the emotional details of another human's experience, fail to develop the abilities needed to "talk that way," my father's shorthand for a huge deficit in his way of relating to me, and probably to everyone else except (possibly) my mother.

Popular culture sees many of these gender differences as biologically given, and to some extent they may be encouraged or deterred by biology. But I have witnessed men, and sometimes been honored to support men, who, with conscious determination, found their way to the skills they had not been taught in their youth or acquired in their gendered roles, men who learned not only how to parent but how to befriend and how to talk. That such change is possible says to me that many gendered differences we assume stem from biology are, like the injuries of race, artifacts of our institutional arrangements. Change systems, and hearts and relationships change as well. System change is what DEI could not address, did not touch, in fact evolved to counteract. Beyond all its other shortcomings, programmatic lessons in overcoming racism colluded with one of the great lies of American mythology, the most basic pretense that we're all equal: the myth of the misnomer society.

13 **The Classless Society**

Healthcare Denying
What the Body Knows

There are moments in history when some disjunction causes people to band together to engage in collective actions they believe will further their shared interests: a riot in Bangladesh, an uproar in a southern American city opposing school desegregation. In earlier chapters, I've mentioned two of my studies looking into such events. What they reveal, singly and together, is a story not only about racial and religious conflict on a social level, but also importantly about class. Studying what collectivities people turned to, how they pursued action, and why the outcomes met or failed their expectations and needs provides a spotlight on a dark place in common understandings of identity-based strife. It is hard to explore hidden caves; it is in just such a place that class in the American story lurks.

I've mentioned in earlier chapters my study of religious enmity. In the late 1960s when I lived in India, I saw close up the injuries of communalism (a word used to identify strife between people of different communities, in this case of Hindu and Muslim identities). In the area where I lived, West Bengal, the two communities coexisted in wary harmony. Before colonial rule, there had been reasonable equity in India: both sides poor agriculturalists living in highly collectivist villages, both communities dealing with rule by foreign masters. Over the years of empire, the British rulers fanned divisions into active competitive animosity, a classic example of "divide and rule." When they left, they left behind two scarred populations as they severed the continent into two new states: India and Pakistan.

United, the area known as Bengal, sharing a common language and culture, had been a land of rivers, mangoes, a special kind of date, and revolutionary elan. But after partition, West Bengal became a Hindu-majority province of India separated from East Bengal, a Muslim-majority province of Pakistan. Horrendous massacres and profound displacements erupted at the time in 1947 when the two new nations became independent. Communal amity in Bengal, as elsewhere on the subcontinent, shattered as huge numbers of Muslims fled east across the newly created international border, crossing paths with Hindus rushing in the opposite direction.

In a further travesty of nation-making, because Muslim-majority regions lay both on the western and eastern sides of the South Asian land mass, Pakistan, in an unwieldy design reflecting political expediency but no sense of coherence, occupied a pasted-together map with the center of power in Punjab separated by a thousand miles of India from the province of East Bengal. Soon after I came to live in Bengal, that eastern region rebelled against its distant overlords and became the independent state of Bangladesh. Our family's specific location in rural India hugged the international border. While our district was majority Hindu, it still contained a significant number of Muslim families.

My neighbors were agreeable people, given to rebellious politics and a collective talent for poetry, music, and dance. Always up for a party, they often joined each other across communal lines for the celebrations of the many holidays in both religious practices. Sometimes certain rituals caused friction, for instance when noisy Hindu processions interrupted solemn Muslim prayers. But by and large people shared the joys, attending each other's holidays, weddings, funerals, and *pujas*. The feeling of commonality remained strong even when strained.

Living in this reality, I gave myself the assignment to understand everything I could about the history of dissension and violence among Bengalis. With the aid of my mother-in-law's extensive memory and vivid storytelling, I learned about times before the hateful communal outbreaks that bloodied the transition from British colonial rule. The first recorded moments of violence between members of the two communities occurred half a century into the colonial experience. Very occasionally after that, the horrific explosion that accompanied independence came as a dramatic surprise. Although they died down after a few years, episodes continued to happen from time to time long afterward, still erupting today. Their legacy and their threat contributes to the Hindu supremacy characterizing political power in India today.

Living in a peaceable village in West Bengal in my twenties, I wondered what enabled the normally kind people I knew as neighbors to transform suddenly into bands of murderous communalists. Having grown up in the Jim Crow

South, I imagined the dynamics that sparked these extremes of identity-based hatred bore some kind of commonality with whatever allowed the Texans I knew, so kind to their children and dogs, to celebrate lynchings and decry in the most hateful terms what they believed to be the dire consequences of something as benign as sending kids of different races to school together. Neither population, Indian nor American, I believed, was better or worse than the other. If common dynamics applied in all such instances, then studying one should shed light on the other. And so eventually I followed my study of South Asian communalism with one of school desegregation in Little Rock, an explosive event that happened at the same time the villagers were rioting in Bengal. That research came to life with the title, *Bitters in the Honey: Tales of Hope and Disappointment Across Divides of Race and Time*. The title tells the story.

In both studies, I could see a common inclination toward one of two narratives to explain these social dissensions. At one moment, people held them to be "age-old animosities." "People just don't get along, never have, never will," ran this theory. But then in another, more modernist version, I frequently heard people blaming opportunistic demagogues for creating hatreds and then playing on them to weaken opponents and keep a grip on power. Recorded history yielded little indication that the first story of either communalism or racism was true. Indeed, centuries of co-existence of the communities in South Asia argued strenuously for a more contemporary genesis. Racism in the American south was clearly grounded in slavery and, undergirding that the Christian Doctrine of Discovery, in historic terms of recent invention and dire racist impact. There was, of course, dramatic evidence in both examples of demagoguery, opportunistic leaders fanning animosities into political success: witness contemporary leaders such as Donald Trump, Viktor Orban, and many others. But that didn't explain why people were susceptible to such manipulations. Leaders cannot lead where followers will not follow. Why did they in India? Why in the American south? Why in so many European nations today?

Both studies focused on a particular moment in the longer history of the strife I sought to understand. Each resulted in many hours of recorded interviews with people who had been involved in that explosive moment. The particular drama I uncovered in Bengal happened a few years after the creation of Pakistan but before the Bangladeshi war of independence.

Most of the population of the area were very poor farmers, some Muslims, others members of a sub-caste of Hindus, all of them very clearly identified as Bengali. Whatever their religious practices or identity, their lives were very similar, and their poverty and experience of subjugation over generations as well. At the time strife broke into public among them, occasioned by a cow belonging to a Muslim family eating a lentil plant belonging to a Hindu one, most of those who had oppressed both groups, typically wealthier Hindu landlords, had moved across the new border to India. With their semi-feudal overlords gone and new access to land temptingly before them, the remaining villagers knew that power at home as well as in some distant capital miles away had shifted, that Muslims, not local Hindus nor distant Europeans now ruled their land. The Hindu villagers I interviewed spoke of fear about a new sense of entitlement they sensed among their Muslim neighbors, but the Muslims told a story of opportunity in this altered political landscape of shifting privileges and authority.

As their accounts rolled out, I noticed something absent. This part of Bengal is famous for its revolutionary politics. Various leftwing political parties were born here and, I knew, continued to be active at the time of the "riot." It was understandable that these hard-working farmers and fishermen would make their best effort to take advantage of new lines of access to influence and resources. But why did they organize on the basis of identity and not shared class circumstances? Why did they organize for action as Hindus and Muslims, not as poor farmers with common interests? Why along communal lines when twenty years later they would unite as Bengalis to wrench independence from Pakistan? People had a choice of identities on which to base solidarity. Nowhere in their stories did I hear justification for having turned on their economic and political peers to slug it out as Hindus and Muslims.

Some Trouble with Cows gave me specific tools with which to further my inquiry: the concept of internalized ideology and the identification of domains within which we construct knowledge. But much more, it shined a sharp light on the invisible: the reality that we do have choices for forming solidarity when faced with a need for political agency.

So what need did the riotous citizens of Little Rock face in the 1950s when all hell broke loose at the doors of Central High School because nine teenagers enrolled in the all-white school?

From Bengal to Arkansas, Contradictions of Power in a Changing World

The year was 1957, the year I left Fort Worth, Texas, for college in the north. Going to college is an ordinary ritual of transition to adulthood for middle-class Americans, but for me it was more of an angry flight. I was sixteen. A few months earlier, in my junior year of high school, I decided I couldn't stand being there anymore. It was a segregated school, several hundred white students who went about their business showing no recognition that they were participating in what to me, an ardent integrationist, was an unendurable quotidian injustice. I had few allies among my classmates, a key one a boy named Sherwin; when he excitedly told me he'd discovered he had enough credits to graduate early and would be leaving at the end of the year, my heart sank. My sister, a little older than me and also my ally, was graduating that June, as were many of our shared friends. I did my own credit accounting, went home to my mother, and announced my intention to leave.

My good mother took a moment to reflect. She knew I was in a constant state of turmoil, faced with the stonewalling authorities of our city and feeling increasingly distressed by the seeming futility of the efforts our little band of integrationists were making. She also knew I was totally bored in school; I had amassed extra credits because I grabbed at any class that seemed interesting in addition to the required curriculum. But she also knew my sister looked forward to her moment of glory as the graduate. I had always outshone her as a scholar; was it right to facilitate one daughter's need at the expense of another's moment in the sun? In the end, she and I met with the principal of the high school, a mild-mannered man I had tormented with my agitations. In my (possibly distorted) memory, he all but cheered and quickly endorsed my leaving.

And so in the fall of 1957, I sat in the library of my college near Boston watching white rioters scream hatred at a terrified Black teenager named Elizabeth Eckford. I watched in horror and grief and rage. Our small band of Fort Worth integrationists had long said to each other, "Once Little Rock integrates, we'll be able to make progress here." Little Rock was supposed to be the border city where desegregation would break the barriers and open other southern schools to progress. Little Rock was supposed to have "good race relations," a peaceable population of people in separate communities but good standing with each other. Central High School would go first; other schools across the South would see their good example and follow suit.

But that's not what happened. Instead, mobs of white people threatened violence toward frightened children on the first day of school. Elizabeth, a shy girl dressed in the ballooning style of skirt of the times, had failed to get a warning from the leaders of her group to gather at a side entrance where the nine Black teens would be escorted by armed guards into the building. Instead, she arrived at the front, smack in the middle of chaos. National news cameras rolled, recording the iconic incident for all the world to see.

Little Rock did not change the south for the better that day, nor in the days and months that followed. Disruption continued throughout that year; the next year the governor, Orval Faubus, closed all the public schools.

Seeking Insight

Watching all this play out on television, one of the first times living history could be watched from the comfort of home, I felt horror and confusion along with anger. As a Jewish child born in the midst of the genocide of people I knew to be *my* people, I learned early in life that very bad things could happen. But as an upper-middle-class, white, American girl from a privileged family, I also imbibed the belief that somehow good would prevail. Now I began to doubt that was true. How urgently I felt the need to understand how both had happened: the Holocaust and riotous resistance to the correction of egregious injustice. I began to think of leaving America, not so much in despair about the state of things there but because I felt ill-equipped to understand that state. I felt as if a cultural fog surrounded my brain, creating boundaries to my consciousness and preventing me from understanding how so much wrongdoing could happen. I left soon after, living in India for many years, returning to the United States at a moment of social upheaval in the early 1970s.

Twenty years later, with insights from Bangladesh in my mind, I set out to use insights from the study of communalism to understand what I could about how the ordinary white people in the United States held racism in their thoughts and feelings. I searched out white people who had been students at Central High the year of the drama. Then, they were seniors in high school;

now they were middle-aged suburbanites nearing retirement. How did they reflect on the gains and losses of their lives? What had they defended then and how had the yields they expected actually been realized? And through it all, how had their beliefs about people of different identities held or changed, and why?

What I learned was that people were disappointed and mystified. Saturated in the mythology of individualism, after their brief walk-on in the drama at Central High, they entertained no thoughts of political organizing. Notions of access to resources on a community level never entered their consciousness. Where the Bengali villagers looked to others of their communal identity as they sought to take advantage of perceived new opportunities, the Little Rock alumnae set out on life's journey coupled but otherwise alone. They did the program they had been given, married soon after high school, produced two or three children, took jobs in corporations, and stayed in them for their lifetimes. They made sacrifices: their employers moved them from one city to another, depending on the needs of the company at the time: free labor, disconnected from land and place, accompanied by wives and children who uncomplainingly followed along.

Except they did complain. The women mourned the loss of community more than anything else in their lives. Sometimes I was able to interview two women together; they lived in places distant from Little Rock and, even though they were friends from childhood, they considered our get-together a rare treat of contact with each other. Mostly, they were too busy, distances too great, husbands and children too unwilling to be with each other in true community. They did visit with neighbors, but like themselves people came and went as husbands' jobs dictated. I asked what they worried about, and they talked about problems with their kids. Their teenagers suffered ennui at school, smoked pot not-so-secretly, had no ambition, no vision of satisfying adult lives. The times were the late 1980s, the age of Ronald Reagan's supply-side economics, of Nintendo and the collapse of communism, of Michael Jackson's "Bad" and the World Wide Web. Teenagers seemed to these moms out of Little Rock to be rootless and depressed—as were they.

The women looked back on their youthful community with nostalgia and confusion, and a good deal of resentment. We did the trip, they said. We married, followed our husbands hither and yon, kept house, made nice with their bosses' wives. But we're worried we won't have enough to retire on. Yes, he'll get a pension, but prices are soaring; will it be enough? And the kids show no sign of growing up and moving on; what's to become of them?! And besides, if we retire, where will we be? No point going back to Little Rock; nobody is there anymore. Where is home now?

Nowhere in these mournful, angry regrets did I hear accusations against the system that had produced their disappointment. Nobody talked about failures of policy or deception by the corporations. Of the dozens of Central High alumnae I interviewed, not one talked about creating intentional community or organizing politically. Where would any protest be aimed anyway? The problem lay somewhere amorphous, mysterious, beyond their ken. What they did see was that some people did get help. "They think that a lot is owed to them," said one woman with a frown, "they do, they think we owe them. And maybe we do, but they're getting more and more, you see it on TV, they're getting, they're getting, they're being given, given, given, and that makes us bitter." What they saw on their TV screens was the political propaganda tropes of the day, representations of Black "welfare queens." They saw news of lawsuits challenging affirmative action programs launched during the previous decade. They saw vicious advertisements for George H. W. Bush's presidential campaign evoking a racist portrait of a Black criminal lurking to prey on innocent white victims.

Confusions of Class Today: Playing the Billionaire Card

Fast forward to the time when I'm now writing. Like Bush's self-serving promotion of a highly prejudicial stereotype, Donald Trump's vendetta against immigrants no doubt exploits the politics of race shamelessly, as did so many representations of his presidential forebearers. But Trump goes even further. By deeming himself to be the *only* person on the face of the earth who *can* solve the nation's problems, he positions himself as that exceptional individual, divinely chosen, to lead the masses out of pain and suffering. Increasingly, as the Trump phenomenon progresses, he transforms himself from candidate to messiah.

If immigrants were not in reality the reason why white middle American folks suffered, if the descendants of enslaved people were also not the cause, if people who challenge gender norms, gay and trans people, if women in the workplace rather than the kitchen are not why men feel abandoned and insecure, then why do these citizens of the land of the free and the equal, of endless opportunity see themselves as so oppressed that they are ready to follow a man of terrible morals and overblown promises, a man proven to be a liar and a philanderer, a man who has already occupied the Oval Office during a pandemic that killed demonstrably more people than needed to die given reasonable leadership: what did almost half the electorate experience in their lives that rendered them so ripe to choose this most unsavory of leaders? What conditions in their lives enabled them to consent to the cruelty of the Trump administration's policies as they inflicted hardship after hardship not only on immigrants and other marginalized groups but also on federal workers of all identities, on poor white people in need of medical care, on ordinary citizens in other lands suffering bombardments by weapons supplied by Washington?

These questions lead us straight to a discussion of class.

If the first of Donald Trump's Inauguration day diktats aimed to erase all awareness of identity-based inequality, the second did the opposite. It focused a bright spotlight on what is usually confined to the shadows, the reality of class in America. All those CEOs of obscenely wealthy tech companies seated where they would inevitably catch the dramatic eye of the television cameras proudly proclaimed a truth: class inhabits the land of equality like a living goliath threatening at every moment to crush ordinary mortals scrambling for existence at its feet. It is a very large and very hard rock on which DEI efforts founder.

What is economic class? Most people in the United States have a hard time defining it. It is not, after all, the categorization we read regularly in our daily media. Class fundamentally speaks to a relationship between the individual and the economy. It is also an identity available to people in most parts of the world but denied to people in America. For Americans to see ourselves as members of a collectivity with a particular relationship to economics is a stretch. When I interview people for a project, I generally include the question, "What class are you?" Very occasionally, somebody will answer, "Working class." That's usually a signal that the person belongs to a labor union to which they feel allegiance, or that they came from that rare family who defined their identity in class terms. Ninety-nine percent of people, however, answer "Middle class." Whether a farmer struggling to survive in a windy Kansas village or a middle manager in a multinational corporation, whether a highly paid surgeon in a nationally renowned hospital or a nurse facing the imminent closure of the rural clinic where she's spent a lifetime working, everyone considers themselves to be part of that amorphous thing American politicians so often appeal to: the middle class. If I were to ask this same question in India or England or Nigeria, I would very likely get a far more nuanced range of answers.

Other cultures are unashamed of class differences. American exceptionalism, however, lies fundamentally in its claim to equal opportunity. That was the lure for the millions who migrated from other lands two hundred years ago, and it is the lure today. Historically, class has been a fundamental fact of social location, something one didn't move on from. Upward mobility was long a unique feature of the new world, a product of massive migration and the unformed economy of a nation-in-the-making. So the disappearance of class as a meaningful social distinction makes some sense. Capitalism, wherever it grew, did in fact offer new opportunities for upward mobility, blurring class barriers in favor of something more—but not universally—fluid.

Class did not disappear, however. It shape-shifted, becoming less easy to name, more complex, but still very relevant to the realities of ordinary people's lives. Class has meant very different things to different thinkers in the past. Marx defined it as a relationship to production: the ruling class were those who owned the means of production, the machines and factories used to produce commodities; the working class or proletariat provided the labor that transformed raw materials into usable commodities but did not own the tools they used nor reap the value of what they produced, a surplus beyond whatever was needed for them to stay alive. This definition lent a clarity to recognizing class distinctions that replicated in very different form the clear lines distinguishing very different classes in the earlier era. Feudalism, for instance, endowed some people with hereditary privileges and obligations unaltered by current circumstances. Everyone could easily identify a member of a noble family as opposed to one who engaged in commerce. People knew which families crafted goods or farmed, and who sent sons into war.

As the nature of economic activity changed with the Industrial Revolution, as production became centralized in burgeoning cities and labor, disassociated from family members, as wages for time spent rather than payment for things made became the norm, lines of class distinction grew steadily more blurred. In theory at least, people could advance from worker to boss, a premise doubted by many workers. But that it seemed possible for anyone loosened hard boundaries of class divisions.

Even more confusing was the question of who actually owned the means of production. By the mid-1900s, corporations had taken the place of identifiable individuals. That corporations in the United States came to be legally defined as individuals further confused the matter. Even those at the top of these hierarchical organizations are vulnerable to a loss of class position under some circumstances. Scandals, hostile takeovers, and other forms of the rough-and-tumble of financial politics occasionally unseat even the mightiest of moguls. If upward mobility is possible, so also is downward.

But there exists a harder reality masked by this seeming fluidity and vagueness. As early as 1956, sociologist C. Wright Mills published his analysis of *The Power Elite*.[1] He identified categories of people populating what he called "the higher circles": celebrities, the very wealthy, chief executives of important companies, leaders of the military, and finally what he called "the political directorate." Each of these categories of people exercises power in different but interlocking ways. Mills contributed a categorization and a vocabulary for recognizing that mystified power works behind the scenes to shape and direct the lives of those he called "mass society": you and me.

While Mills' detailed analysis is both engrossing and enlightening, it also obscured what popular society was intent on ignoring at the time of publication. I first encountered the book in a sociology class at Brandeis University, where I attended college starting in 1957. Here was a place where "book learning" and the consensus among the people surrounding me conflicted painfully with my lived experience. Nowhere does Mills address either the vitriolic racism I heard at every turn in political and social contention for power in Texas. Even as I read *The Power Elite*, I watched on television the governor of Little Rock turn from a lukewarm integrationist to a vociferous rouser of the racist mob at the door of Central High School. Mills quoted a long piece from the NY *Times* that described how then president Eisenhower was groomed for television celebrity by professionals; I read it while I agonized over Eisenhower's refusal to authorize military intervention in Little Rock, the only authority able to protect the nine Black students enrolled in the school. When that order was finally forced from the television-aware president, the Nine were able to attend classes but left with little protection inside the school as their peers either harassed or ignored them and the mobs continued their ugly opposition outside the windows.

While these particular events happened after Mills' book was published, there were many other kinds of evidence of both the prominence and the exclusion from power of Americans of color and of women. Even on the level of celebrity, how did Mills manage to overlook Black musicians and athletes? Perhaps he could have been unaware of groundbreaking people like Little Richard, Ray Charles, or Ella Fitzgerald. Jazz defined a community of people of color, often sidelined however much the enormous talents of its artists were acknowledged and appreciated by some white critics and fans. But Nat King Cole, a singer as mainstream in my youth as Frank Sinatra or Bing Crosby?

That Black stars and others of color were overlooked by a sociologist, even one as perceptive as C. Wright Mills, fits seamlessly into the white culture I was experiencing by then. The civil rights movement was well in progress. A year before *Power Elite* was published, during the time Mills presumably worked on the manuscript, Rosa Parks held her bus seat in Montgomery, Alabama, and the Montgomery Bus Boycott was launched. That movement propelled Martin Luther King to national prominence. So C. Wright Mills must have known both of Black celebrities and Black political leaders. That he did not define them as part of the power system, however, was not a mistake. That he makes no mention in his otherwise important book, though, says something eloquent in its omission, suggesting wrongly that their absence is not an essential part of the story of class in America, then and now.

Intersecting Lines of Class and Race: The Matching Cases of Prison and Maternal Death

Almost three-quarters of a century later, what has changed at that intersection of race and class power? Any assessment must include two stark facts standing at its center: the incarceration of Black and Brown men, and deaths in childbirth among Black women. There is a trope in today's right-leaning culture that racism is a thing of the past, that the election of Barack Obama, a Black president, proves we live in post-racist times. Trump doubled down on that contention, doing his best to erase all history or mention of discrimination. These easily accessible statistics dramatically challenge such a contention:

At the end of 2023, the Bureau of Justice Statistics, a federal agency, reported that 1,250,000 people were incarcerated in federal and state prisons, all but a very few males. When rates of incarceration are calculated, meaning how many people of a certain demography as a proportion of that group's total in the population at large, Black people go to prison at six times the rate of white people. As I write, just under 40 percent of the prison population in both federal and state institutions is Black, compared with about 13 percent of the US population. A comparable comparison for Hispanic people is also skewed but far less dramatically: about 30 percent incarcerated; about 20 percent of the population. For white people, the disproportion is in the other direction: under 40 percent of the prison count in the context of 60 percent of the general population.[2]

These comparisons are often explained by a long list of discrepancies in who gets arrested for what activities (such as drug dealing or larceny); who gets approved for pre-trial diversion programs; who is convicted and who is acquitted; how much longer sentences tend to be for people of color than for white people; and who gets paroled and when. At each of these steps, racism steps in to disadvantage the disadvantaged.

But these intrusions into procedural justice ripen in an even more damning context of alienation and violence. Label Black men "dangerous," put them at risk of violence both from the state in the form of the police and from other men, endow them with a high capacity for camaraderie (because team sports are allowed and danger on the streets induces membership in gangs) and a low capacity for intimacy (because they are men), and you've created a perfect recipe for crafting a population in prison. The ingredients map all the elements I've touched on in earlier chapters, starting with the ways young boys of all races but especially those who are Black struggle from the moment they set foot in a schoolroom. While girls of five may be more inclined to sit still, whether because they are already socialized to obedience or because their brains have already developed the pathways that enable inactivity, boys are way more likely to experience the "sit still" command as torture. In charge of over-stuffed classrooms and enjoined to do the impossible and keep the kids quiet, teachers clamp down. If they are also saturated in stereotypes of Black boys as troublemakers, then their disciplinary impulses are more likely to turn punitive. By the time these children reach high school, they may be sullenly rebellious and diagnosed with ADHD and oppositional defiant disorder. As my teenage informant in Little Rock so eloquently expressed, they may also have concluded that they are bad students, not recognizing that they are forced to occupy an imprisoning social environment where they are treated as bad students.

Meanwhile, in the streets beyond school they may live in an atmosphere of violence and fear. Parents, themselves stressed to breaking point, struggle to sustain loving care for others and, in their own fear for the survival of their sons, resort to punishment in futile attempts at control. In the boys' world, however, safety lies elsewhere. In Chapter 3, we saw Dr. Hasshan Batts' analysis of the route by which these kids' need for security morphs into gang membership. Already having internalized the identity "troublemaker," they play to the label at the same time that the authorities outside them collude in fear and bias, assuming their bonded groups to be gangs. That label plunges them into the polluted waters of criminality. Whether they actually engage in outlaw activities or not, the framing constitutes a worldview. Combined with the reality of exclusion from opportunities for sustainable careers, they may reasonably turn to the one segment of the economy available to them: drug dealing.

I have not previously discussed why people peddling illegal substances find so many customers: the many Americans, no matter what their complexion, who turn to street drugs for relief, pleasure, and sometimes companionship. But everything I've written about alienation points people in that direction, side by side with the use of legal drugs prescribed by the psychiatric industry. Why not pop a pill, or eventually inject a vein, when life seems bleak and oppressive? So the one economic activity that may be open to the Black kids, now so thoroughly alienated from legal well-being as well as so thoroughly excluded, is the drug trade. Is there a mystery, then, that the nation finds itself with one of the largest incarcerated populations in the industrialized world, heavily complexioned Black?

Dying in Childbirth, a Black Woman's Peril

Meanwhile, in this most highly developed of industrial countries, where the medical community boasts itself to be among the most advanced available anywhere in the world, fully half of the women who die in childbirth are Black. Another 12 percent are Hispanic and almost 11 percent Asian. Compare those figures for white maternal mortality in a society where white women make up almost sixty percent of the female population: 14.5 percent.[3] The rate for Black women is more than double the overall US rate.

Much research has been dedicated to explaining this discrepancy. Results highlight obvious factors lying at the confluence of race and class: poorer women get less medical care all along through pregnancy and in childbirth. Beyond those economic metrics (and let's pause for a moment to bemoan the fact that care and money are so closely associated), two other more subtle dynamics show up. Medical staff tend to exercise more doubt when Black women report pain or other manifestations of trouble. And the stressors of racism in daily life, at work, on the streets, and virtually everywhere else, show up as cortisol changes during pregnancy that negatively impact the well-being of a fetus. Add to those stressors the strains when Black fathers are absent, whether because they're in prison or imprisoned in the traps and roles I've touched on.

The Power Elite: Still White After All These Years

For all the effort in the intervening decades, for all the growth of a Black middle class and a grounded Latino community growing more politically conservative, true access to power still remains dramatically a white male monopoly. It is true that African American representation in Congress has increased to approximately mirror the number in the US population, the result of some brilliant political organizing. Hispanic representation remains about two-thirds. Interestingly, it is the proportion of women that lags significantly behind; slightly over a quarter of the House and Senate combined are female while women comprise over half the population.

More tellingly still is the proportion of top executives of Fortune 500 companies who are white men. Those billionaires seated at the Trump inauguration symbolize the reality that who controls money largely controls the levers of government. Over twenty years from the turn of the current century, women in that club increased from two to fifty-two. Most of these newcomers were white; the proportion of people of color of either gender among Fortune 500 CEOs remained fewer than forty. Only 1 percent were Black, 2.4 percent South or East Asian, and 3.4 percent Latino.[4]

Statistics tell only a thin slice of the story. How ordinary people perceive power reflects their own sense of their life choices. The great myth of the United States is the American Dream: the idea that anyone can rise from poverty to occupy the highest heights. For much of the history of the nation, rags to riches stories animated the psyches of its people—at least, of its white people. Read as the opportunity through hard work to achieve a family, home ownership, and a secure retirement, it is the vision that people from Little Rock told me had guided their life choices in the 1950s but rang hollow thirty years later. Let's note that for African Americans, the animating dream was quite different, not a white picket fence but Martin Luther King's famous dream in 1963: "I have a dream that my four little children will one day live in a nation where they will not be judged by the color of their skin but by the content of their character."

Today, what remains of either Dream? In 2024, the Pew Research Center asked Americans that question. Around half of the people surveyed thought the American Dream was still attainable, but over a third of African Americans believed it once was but no longer, and a tenth believed that it never had been.

Building Connection to Reclaim Humanity

Another world is not only possible, she is on her way. On a quiet day, I can hear her breathing.

Arundhati Roy, from a speech at the World Social Forum
in Porto Allegre, Brazil, 1/27/2003

14 **How Change Happens**
When We're Not
Even Looking

How's the weather where you are today? What calamities dramatize the forecast? Nothing shouts more eloquently the news of a system at the breaking point than the global climate crisis.

What does the weather have to do with overcoming injustice and ensuring to all humans the lives we want and deserve? In today's world, everything. I want to connect those dots for a few reasons. First, I don't hear a lot of optimism about prospects for progress toward equality and justice. On the contrary, people in my world, although out in the streets protesting and coming together in local organizations, are discouraged. My friend Y's question at the very beginning of this book suggests to me exasperation, fatigue, disappointment, and also determination and hope. In paradoxical ways, though, the responsibility for building a better world does not rest solely on the actions we take. Dynamics built into the ways that societies develop also create the means by which particular forms of social organization come apart at the seams. In the ideal—and here is where human intentions and actions do matter—what then bursts forth is a qualitative improvement on what went before.

In very simplified form, this is basic Marxist theory. Societies constantly create new technology to meet changing needs. Hunter-gatherer societies tame fire and invent agriculture to produce greater quantities of food capable of sustaining increasing populations, which in turn grow beyond what the tools at hand enable people to produce. During the process when planting and harvesting replaced hunting and gathering, migratory bands of people probably discovered the benefits of settling in constructed habitats. Now, as a need for more land to grow more food for more surviving humans and their newly domesticated animals increases, perhaps friction develops with other groups settled nearby. Labor differentiates under newly evolving demands: women probably were the first farmers, learning to plant seeds they gathered in the wild while men primarily covered the tasks of hunting. But as the technology of food production advances and more land comes under cultivation, men do more of that work while women, given the biology of birth and nursing, and perhaps need for their craft skills, become more confined to domesticity. We don't really know where patriarchy first arose. Many years ago, I did a brief study of tribal peoples in South Asia. Surprised by the rich variety of social arrangements from one group to another, I found some that were matriarchal and others that practiced female infanticide and polygamy. The most isolated of them, the Onges of the Andaman Islands, still shared power in the most fluid ways imaginable. What we do know is that both work assignments and gender dynamics almost universally grew more separate. They also became infused with domination. Did women object to their increasing confinement to home? Was that what started humanity down the troubled path to patriarchal violence? We can only speculate, not know.

It is evident, though, that through evolution and revolution, social relations have bent and shifted over the centuries, transforming to meet new needs under new conditions. Manufacturing replaces craft, giving rise to urban concentrations where industrial production processes are worked by an urbanized labor force. Those lands most highly industrialized colonize and exploit others where both raw materials and consumer markets for commodities are plentiful. Insofar as societies can be ranked into more or less industrialization, those still primarily agricultural where communal relations prevail sometimes leapfrog past those with systems rendered stable, and consequently static, by elites determined to protect their privileges.

What I mean to sketch here is a dynamic flowing through human history, in order to view the present moment through that lens. Although some people dispute it, there is very wide agreement that the global economy has succeeded in creating technologies that are now destroying the earth. One might think that the first order of imperative actions for those with the greatest stake in advanced capitalism—those who most profit from it— would be to prevent that contradiction from blowing us all to perdition. Instead, we see those in power, certainly in the United States but to a greater or lesser extent on a global scale, opting to keep the machinery of capitalism humming in order to protect what they see, with extraordinarily limited vision, as their interests: they are, after all, living creatures who stand to be wiped out along with the rest of us.

Indeed, in the early days of the second Trump administration, almost every action taken by the federal government served to heighten the contradiction. By eliminating programs to advance technologies for environmentally protective energy sources, for instance, while promoting fossil fuels instead, precisely those substances known to create the problem, officials making these decisions demonstrate a capacity for denial that brings us ever closer to the brink of cataclysm. As climate disasters tear across the land, flooding communities here, burning others there, carrying yet more away in monster tornadoes and hurricanes, the central government defunds agencies to both predict these events and to restore communities after devastation.

Meanwhile, wealth is transferred by many different means to the wealthy from the poor even more stridently than by any other American administration for almost a hundred years. And so the contradiction between need and policy, between the social good and satisfying the greed of billionaires, grows ever more extreme. There are so many metaphors that could be applied here, none exactly apt. A chick growing large enough to finally break through its shell? Too gentle. A tadpole growing lungs that finally succeed in liberating the adult frog from the water? Too organic. A house in disrepair that finally falls down?

This last metaphor has some reality for me. My father was a capable home repairman; because he could fix whatever needed maintenance, he persistently believed he should. But he didn't. Always more interested in his medical practice, or his involvement in that hardest of causes, Democratic politics in Texas, or with a late-in-life discovery of talent as a portrait painter, he looked away from the clogged kitchen plumbing that remained and the wooden deck in the backyard as it grew perilously rotten. We adult children did what we could to fix this or that. But when my father died and the house went on the market, the new owners tore it down and built anew.

So too mature capitalism is the means of its own undoing. While it destroys the planet and marches triumphantly over the unheralded needs of its ordinary people, social dissent grows, nature rebels, economies crash. When the center, growing ever smaller, always less aware, ever more selfish, can no longer hold, things get worse before they get better. Trump himself can be seen as the manifestation of a process already far advanced.

The electoral tilt to the right in 2024 that returned Trump to the White House gave political form to what so many Americans knew: the system wasn't working for them. Having given up on the American Dream, stinging from unguarded contempt from liberal thinkers in academic and popular settings, resentful of what they experienced as tone, language, and thought policing by hired DEI consultants and mainstream media, ready for repressed racist suspicions to be set free, people voted an authoritarian, self-styled king posing as a savior into office. Caught in a Hobbesian trap, the choices they faced between "liberals" who did them no good as their factory towns collapsed, their farms defaulted to huge agriculture companies, their children languished on drugs and unemployment, and their elders died of medical inattention; and on the other side, a self-proclaimed billionaire who decried everything they blamed for their ills and promised he'd take matters into his own magical hand and save them. Instead, his early acts in office all did the opposite: tariffs that increased daily costs, program elimination that left them without access to government assistance, and funding policies that undercut their schools, their medical resources, and the safety of their roads and skyways.

Trump can be held responsible for a lot of harm. But he is only the most extreme consequence so far of the heightening contradiction between social well-being and technological advancement. How far can the politics of capitalism stretch before everything collapses? What would seem to predict a breaking point are two primary things: environmental disaster, as I've already said, and also a precipitous decline of the birthrate in advanced capitalist countries around the world combined with medical advances that enable an older and older population to survive and require care.

Formula for Social Change: Heating Planet, Chilling Fertility, and a Surplus of Old People

If nothing else were happening, environmental degradation by itself would be enough to augur social collapse. For many of you reading these words, no argument is needed. The globe has passed the tipping point predicted by many climate scientists to mean irreversible damage. As if to demonstrate to the skeptical, dramatic weather patterns would seem to prove the claim. Heat waves in the United States and Europe kill elderly people. Southern lands boil while lethal cold forces public events (such as Donald Trump's Inauguration) indoors. Extreme hurricane activity is under watch in the

Atlantic Ocean. Arctic sea ice has reached a historic low for the time of year as sea levels rise and rise. Tornadoes tear through parts of North America where they've never before been seen. Downpours simultaneously flood places in the America, Africa, South Asia, and more. Violent weather interrupts travel, trade, and construction everywhere. Global warming afflicts people across all boundaries, including national, racial, and class.

While individuals and groups may adopt practices to ameliorate these changes, it remains obvious that only federal and global level policies can make a significant difference. Yet democratic societies and autocratic ones all so far fail to take the necessary steps. The mechanisms for protecting populations are so evidently failing as the momentum of economic practices that are well known to promote warming take precedence over the well-being of living beings. It is precisely the advances, having given vitality to global capitalism's exploitation of nature, that now sound a death knell for the planet. So essential have fossil fuels been to the ability of technology to advance over the past two centuries, from locomotion to a rapacious need for electricity, from sustaining huge urban populations to using insanely poisonous chemicals in order to produce enough food to feed an expanding population, that Mother Nature now demands the price for modernity. To withdraw fossil fuels and substitute wind, solar, or other non-toxic forms of energy means retooling industries. In private hands, these businesses rely on producing profits to keep the capitalist ecology of money flowing. Here in living technicolor is the contradiction of which Marx wrote: the success of the system is its own undoing.

For decades, since the end of the Second World War, capitalist societies have managed to balance two necessities of the system: to provide enough resources to the populace to keep people alive and sufficiently satisfied, or mystified, to accept the status quo; and to extract from the system ever-expanding profits to keep the machinery of the economy humming by making investors increasingly enriched. In the early post–Second World War years, high taxation and sufficient regulation of industry helped to maintain a compromise. A central mechanism of that management dynamic was the labor movement. A wide range of political ideology animated different unions, from the idealism of the west coast longshoremen to the get-what-you-can-however-you-can of the plumbers. But all of them provided a mechanism by which workers' wages could be negotiated sufficiently to keep labor conflict at a workable minimum.

In the 1980s when Ronald Reagan was elected, however, things changed. Reagan's first act in office was to destroy the Air Controllers' Union, a decisive move in collapsing what few recognized at the time to be a fragile house of cards. As the unions' power to represent labor crashed, so too did regulations. Fiscal policy, too, set profit-takers free to prosper. In retrospect, we can see that these policy acts followed a path coinciding with the ambition of a Christian conservative intention to recast American society in their image. In other advanced capitalist countries, now also leaning heavily to the right, the specific dynamics varied, but the direction coincided.

Now that the grand compromise of the 1950s has vanished, young people face unique dilemmas. Both emotional and financial burdens of the environmental crisis confront them with supercharged decisions about their futures. With no good visions of the future apparent, many choose not to reproduce. Why bring children into a world of disaster, with future existence in doubt and, on a more quotidian plane, where increasing expenses of life collude with the collapse of community to leave parents far too burdened and alone for child rearing to look like a lot of fun?

In much of the industrialized world, fertility rates are falling below the point at which population remains stable: 2.1 births per reproductive age woman. Japan, Italy, South Korea, and other countries already see their labor forces strained by the shortage of young workers. On the other side of the equation, the older generation enjoys the fruits of advanced medical technology, living longer and inevitably needing more care. With family size at a low ebb of one or two children per child-bearing couple, who is to provide that care?

In the United States and some other nation states, what alleviates the crunch is immigration: for some years, American population growth has been entirely reliant on newcomers, a reliable source of labor to keep us all fed, clothed, cleaned, and otherwise serviced. What happens, then, when a nativist movement blocks the migratory process? Little wonder that the supremacy of that movement as I write combines with a natalist one—which, however, creates a significant clash with women's rights and adds wind to the sails of a Christian fundamentalist ideology that envisions the savior of society to be a heteronormative family, producing babies and corralling women's labor in the home caring for both children and elders.

Anti-immigrant and pro-baby politics both reflect and drive contradictions in the social sphere where economy and psychology come together. I've seen in my own practice how much the uncertainties of employment drive workers in technology into psychiatric territory. What gets diagnosed as anxiety disorder seems to me to be a sane and inevitable consequence of overwork, super competition, and constant job changes. Either they work for mega-corporations like Google and Microsoft, or they take the challenge of startups. In the former, despite all the perks and promises, employees often find conditions intolerable: long hours, intense pressure to produce, mystification of worker relations when "teams" have no clear instruction for sharing power, working collaboratively, or overcoming competitive strains cultivated by unclear role definitions and reward structures, as well as by the education system that produced these workers in the first place. Meanwhile, before Washington shut down DEI altogether, efforts to insert racial and gender diversity into these institutions often backfired; people were recruited and then plunged into poorly functioning social systems with no capacity to recognize discrimination on the floor, nor to do anything about it if recognized. People of color and women came and left, aggrieved and upset, brimming with mental health needs. Still today, startups sometimes inspire creative participation and high hopes for wealth for some of these distressed workers, but most new businesses fail to survive or to deliver if they do. Stressed constantly to raise funds, young innovators find themselves required to cater to the power of venture capitalists and other investors, no more able to meet the needs of their staff than any other institution on the horizon.

All this human distress manifests broad trends in the structure of production and work. As regulation of industry weakens under constant political assault, as environmental conditions grow more and more extreme, as the workforce becomes more insecure and, with the added factor of individualism, more isolated, these factors collude in the dominance of a tiny elite group of executives and other leaders. The extremes of resource distribution cannot remain hidden. The richest 1 percent in the world now owns 25 percent of all wealth. Whether it's about housing or medical care or good quality education, the unfairness that some have so much and so many have so little cannot be hidden. I suggest that capitalism has survived many earlier crises because that injustice has been confused by myths of endless opportunity. As long as people are convinced by individualism that the fault lies not in the stars but in themselves, that they too could join the elite ranks of the billionaire class if they continue to try, then they do not stamp their collective foot and say, No more!

And what then? That large segments of the white populace idolize a wealthy capitalist who constantly raises an alarm that brown people are replacing whites is no accident. Trump is a progression, not an anomaly. Many hardcore MAGA adherents live in parts of the country in sharp economic decline. Large corporations controlling vast tracts of land have for decades been replacing family farms, which suffer the further degradation of the climate crisis. Mining communities lost vitality long ago, and those in coal country impose the added indignity of requiring miners to blast veins more deeply embedded in rock, causing not only black lung, a condition of older miners, but also silicosis, a potentially fatal condition that shows up in much younger men. Meanwhile, funding for rural hospitals grows ever more constrained, causing institutions serving small communities to close. Some years ago, I spent time in a village in western Kansas. Their hospital hung by a thin thread of disappearing funding; their high school had closed a few years earlier; they relied for police protection on a tiny force housed several villages and miles away. The only doctor in town was an immigrant enrolled in a program to work for a few years in an underserved area as a route to legal status in the United States. While villagers, all of them white, feared and disliked other immigrants, they adored their young physician, who hailed from the Middle East.

Despotism or Revolution? Tale of Collapsing Alternatives

Desperation orients people either to despotism or to revolution. Historically, often the wave moves one way before shifting to the other. What do the trends I've sketched here portend for the future? Your guess is as good as mine, but I'm imagining that young people will not tolerate how tightly the bind squeezes them into submission to oppression. The Kansas villagers mourned the loss of their children to the cities; meanwhile, urban youth, immersed in an ecology of media, cannot literally leave—where would they go?—but some of them may confound older generations with other ways to reject dominance, at least on a cultural level. Many of those leaning left reject binaries, especially of gender. They confront their elders with grammatical radicalism, insisting on using a non-gendered plural for a singular person. They reject monogamy and with it, conventional families. They seek collaborative ways of living and working, sometimes even returning to the land to start experimental farming enterprises. All these rejections of the world they've inherited are not, of course, shared by all young people. On the other side, some tilt more heavily into the older conventionalities and conservative politics.

Either way, the pressures so widely experienced reinforce tendencies to cluster with one's "tribe." In America, people of color already often (but not always!) know who that is. Oppression describes the boundaries of "my people." Also, both African Americans and Latino Americans often have access to organized communities in the form of churches: Black Protestant ones for the former, Catholic ones for the latter, although increasingly also evangelical Christians. Many of these congregations embrace socially liberal theologies (liberation theology in the Catholic Church, for example) and institutional forms that maintain independence from elitism within their denominations (Black churches especially). White Americans, however, lacking defined grounds for solidarity, are more apt to experience a generational divide. Even within families, younger people form oppositional cultural identities that defy convention, while older people turn more inward. While the young reach out, the old draw the boundaries of a shaky identity more tightly around themselves. The young innovate while the old protect. When the time comes to vote, people under thirty lean left, those over sixty list hard right.[1]

What then becomes of the demands of a declining population in the face of blocked immigration and the need for a workforce that grows ever more disaffected with working conditions? Add to this a political and cultural thread attempting to pressure women to produce more babies. It's not hard to foresee some very fiery gender friction on the horizon. Their mothers and grandmothers having fought hard for women's rights for a century, young women may not formulate their rights so clearly in gendered terms. But they know their rights. It is impossible for me to imagine my sixteen-year-old granddaughter submitting to the bedroom and the kitchen under the direction of any male. She may not feel a need to fight for equality right now—she just assumes it. But she's soon to meet a different reality, out in the adult world. If Mia is representative, resistance to the right-wing agenda for the coming decades is likely to be deep and furious.

15 Reclaiming Vision, Exercising Agency

Creating a Beloved Multicultural Community

While history rolls inexorably onward, taking its own twists and time, we ordinary people can't stand still. We have a crucial part to play in the change that is brewing. Change happens on both grand and minute scales I've described, but every moment of historical transformation contains within it very many small acts by many ordinary people, performed on a daily basis and coalescing in large dramatic moments of protest and reconstitution. I've written about how the Trump phenomenon rested on years of preparation involving acts both small and large. So too do those of us who crave a better world need to be building the one we wish to inhabit even as we labor to birth her into existence.

There are two levels on which we need to operate: one is building solidarity wide and sturdy enough to challenge power; the other is practicing the future in the present. Progressive political and community organizers know far more than I about the former; I have thoughts to share about the latter. Where the two come together, however, is in the way people treat each other when organizing for social change. Because I am old enough to have seen a lot of grief produced by radicals with hearts and minds in the right place but little knowledge of how truly to collaborate, especially in multicultural settings, I start with a critique of the traditional left.

In a different time when hardship cried out for revolution, Berthold Brecht wrote a poem called "To Posterity":[1]

For we knew only too well
Even the hatred of squalor
Makes the brow grow stern.
Even anger against injustice

Makes the voice grow harsh. Alas, we
Who wished to lay the foundations of kindness
Could not ourselves be kind.

When patriarchy kills the emotional part of male children, as bell hooks bemoans, the one emotion it still allows is anger. Anger feels powerful, and anger glides easily into unkindness, and also violence. Is violence necessary to enact social change? Certainly, the old left thought it was. Power, it was widely thought, will never be relinquished without physical struggle.

Today, we live in a time when the means to do violence, like all technologies, have become so monstrous, so gargantuan, that its possibilities defy its usefulness. By that I mean that we the people do not have the means to win a war of arms against the massive capacity of the state to do violence to us. So if the old model of revolution is an uprising of an armed populace, what is the new vision? Answers to the question nest in how we make use of technologies and knowledge not available to activists until very recently.

Digital technology, most obviously, allows for immediate communication across all lines of separation. Creativity inspired, enabled, and shared by social media both challenges consent to injustice and stimulates powerful means to organize collective action. Uprisings that have toppled governments in recent years made good use of these technologies, witness the Arab Spring as far back as 2011. Ultimately, though, what opened the doors to change were people massed in such enormous numbers that short of massacring millions, states stood helpless before the onslaught. We saw that most recently in Bangladesh. A youth rebellion there, initiated by teenagers aggrieved by changes to academic requirements, grew exponentially, gathering into its ranks many other people unhappy about many other issues, until in a very short time the repressive leadership in power, a regime that had seemed invulnerable for many years, fled the country. Revolutions often start where least expected. After years of organizing by Lenin, Trotsky, and others in Russia, while, in exile, the leaders debated strategies, one day women factory workers in Petrograd rose up to demand better conditions and more bread. Laying down tools in unison, they walked out. But they didn't stop there. Going from factory to factory, they called out their menfolk and launched the Russian Revolution.[2]

But if the revolutionaries of an earlier era could not be kind, neither could the societies they birthed. I think of this equation not as a philosophical question about means and ends but instead as a question of process and emergence. On a very different level, in the conflict transformation work we've done now for decades, we know that the process by which change is made creates the quality of the change that results. Regimes installed by revolutionary processes very often find themselves resorting to authoritarian means to control the rebellious populations who handed them power, thereby betraying the revolutionary mandate they've been handed. If the new order we seek is one in which power is genuinely shared, what do we know about what that even means? In real life, how rare are the opportunities to experience power sharing in any part of life? Hierarchy and competitiveness are the norm, cooperation and equality a rarity.

Let me say that another way: as we work and, yes, fight for a different world, we are given a unique opportunity to learn how to be in the world we create—and indeed a responsibility to use the collective processes essential to building power to launch a new society as a place to learn how to be egalitarian. The more we practice in the now what we want in the future, the more likely it becomes that we'll know how to be in the future the way we wish to be.

That way, for me, is in respectful and truthful equality. I'm not talking about some airy-fairy wish that we all be nice people. All equality must be grounded in very specific behaviors, starting with honesty; if we don't have knowledge, then we don't have the power to articulate and negotiate our needs. But too often we've been taught, through internalized judgment or fear, to minimize needs, to compromise our interests even before we begin to negotiate them. So if the first step is honest expression, the second is collaborative problem solving to find ways to achieve what we and others, equally, need. If I stand in support of your well-being and you of mine, then even when we differ in end goals, we stand a good chance of discovering something that's even better for us both. Multiply that picture by a community process, with lots of help from lots of other people, and multiply that to ever greater collections of people, and social change is happening right now, in the process of working toward it.

If we pledge to speak truth to each other, including the truth of our visions and needs and interests, if then we promise to work out differences with commitment to everyone's satisfaction with the outcome, then we have a lot to learn and to practice. Individualistic, competitive capitalist culture doesn't teach these skills. But every conflict, every disagreement, every challenge to moving forward together can become another lesson plan for learning what we need to know. If that agenda stands at the center of all organizing, then we're speeding toward that world Arundhati Roy identified: "Another world is not only possible, she is on her way. On a quiet day, I can hear her breathing."

On a practical level, here are some of the ways we can practice in the present:

- Every day, we can spend a few minutes imagining the ways we'd truly like life to be. This practice pushes back against normalization. It strips the veil of cultural hegemony from obfuscations of the dominant culture. We're told that Obamacare is an achievement, but what if we aimed higher: why not readily available, free health support to everyone, no insurance companies second-guessing doctors? What if good water, unpolluted air, fresh foods were all resources we took for granted—not only for a few who go to great lengths to find those conditions, but for everyone? What if every parent were surrounded by a community of support, present daily to play with, care for, transport, and generally grandparent every child?

- We can courageously lean into conflict. Americans are notoriously both litigious and conflict averse, as is much of the rest of the world. We outsource our conflicts to courts and other arbitrators. But if we engaged discord skillfully, if we asked for help and embraced conflict as a time of learning and change, we stand to gain not only peaceful lives but an ability to craft progress attuned to our human needs. And in the process, we'd find ourselves enjoying truly equal relationships with supposed adversaries, while building more and more solidarity, across all sectors, identities, geographies, interests, ideologies, and whatever else threatens to weaken our collective voice for justice.

- To the greatest extent possible, we can learn to participate in relationships that truly embody equality. What that means in practice is radical; we know a lot about what inequality looks like from the work over decades on multiculturalism, but we know very little about true equality. So this goal means learning as we go. It is the essence of birthing the new order inside the house of the old one.

Let's flesh out each of these actions.

I start with vision because to reclaim this essence of our humanity underlies and strengthens everything else we do. The analyses and stories I've offered in this book mean to demystify the ways we get recruited into participating in injustice and, along the way, relinquishing our own rights and needs.

That last point is the point of my analysis: all these factors, each one interacting with all the others, end up mystifying the hardships we endure, turning us against each other, isolating us in dysfunctional family units housed in dysfunctional structures, and sending us off to earn a living doing meaningless work in oppressive, alienated organizations. Not seeing alternatives, we consent to these insane, and insanity-inducing, conditions.

But that is not the end of the story. At the same time people resist, in small ways and large, from stealing paper clips to organizing massive strikes. I am indebted to Jim Scott for his concept of insurrectionary calisthenics.[3] The small transgressive actions we take from time to time—crossing a street against the light, cheating on our income tax return, adding minutes to our allotted lunch break, gaming the system to get financial aid, and all the other creative acts of defiance we do—when done with consciousness of what we're actually rebelling against, strengthen muscles needed at the critical time of mass resistance. For one thing, they demonstrate that resistance is possible; for another, they nurture a certain cynicism about the rules that can easily morph into more collective and political forms. My list of elements amounts to a recipe for consent to unjust social systems; the mechanism of consent is the internalization of a belief in powerlessness. Let's revoke consent! Believing that a better world is possible opens the door to imagining what that world could be. We all had the power of imagination once upon a time. It hasn't vanished, only been suppressed. Let it loose now!

Reclaim Vision

Any system that seeks to rob people of agency begins with the suppression of imagination. If Mia gives up in the moon and if Adi's curiosity about an adult friend is labeled inappropriate and shut down, then why would either child continue to yearn and to wonder? Right along with imagination, we also lose the compassion for others that results. No longer can we walk in another's shoes as we grow away both from the creative ability to write their story and also from intimate knowledge of our own feelings. This loss of access to the emotional self lives in the tissues of the physical self. We grow armored against the discomforts of oppression; why feel things if we believe ourselves helpless to remedy them? I think of trauma as powerless engraved into body tissue by violent acts. In the moment of that experience in the past, we may well have been powerless—but not in the present. Being safe may mean speaking out, calling for help, locking windows, and other physical acts. Believing we have the power to be safe is a practice encouraged and supported by community.

Over time, our capacity to envision the ideal collapses under the weight of others' judgments and coercion. "Don't be silly," we are warned, apparently a terrible thing to be. "That's just pie in the sky," we're warned when we express our fondest dreams. "You'll outgrow all that adolescent idealism," I was told. But I have not; wouldn't it be wonderful if there were in fact pie in the sky? I love pie. What's wrong with "being silly," including having fun with imaginative fantasies? If we can't imagine it, how will we ever create it? How many ways did your grownups insist, "You can't lasso the moon!"? They were wrong. For sure, if you can't wish for it, you'll never have it. Mia didn't literally capture the moon, but both she and I had a whole lot of fun. And we did write a great little illustrated children's book called "Mia and the Moon." Grown now to another magical age on the cusp of adulthood, she's not shy about wishing even while she's practical and highly skilled at pursuing the things that matter to her.

So fantasize! Get together with friends and spin tall tales of possible worlds. There is little as productive as creative group think. We stimulate each other to move beyond the boundaries of imagination when we dream together. (If you want a few prompts, take a look at Ruha Benjamin's lovely book, *Imagination: A Manifesto*. She also offers a cool workbook online.)

Embrace Conflict

If we think of conflict as a revelation of a contradiction within some human society, whether a population of two or of millions, a moment when problems have reached boiling point and demand to be addressed, then conflict becomes synonymous with transformation. If we can't face dissension with courage, courtesy, honesty, and imagination, then we are doomed to be constantly mired in strife. How we deal with the big conflict of social change is informed by how we deal with the quotidian conflicts in all our relationships. In this realm, practice is essential. There is much we can theorize about conflict, but every experience is different. We can only learn what we need to know through practice.

Useful principles emerge from the work we've done over recent years in mediating conflicts, many of them based in identity differences. First, all conflict is on some level about power. And so every process of working through conflict is a mini revolution, a transformation of power relations. By power, I mean the multiple realms in which we experience agency, an ability to act, starting with an internalized belief in what's possible for us and what's not.[4] Given the limitations confronting virtually every modern child—isolation, tapped-out parents, sedentary schools, high-risk public spaces, and so on—more often than not we come to maturity believing "I can't" rather than "That's possible!" We give up before we begin, or we start out fighting before we need to. When I mediated my home community, a story recounted in my book *The Bernal Story*, at the outset each side told me, "We never win!" As an informed guess, there was a good deal of reality to that belief. Mired in an oppositional, zero-sum conflict, neither side would have "won." Worked through with respect, care, and perseverance, though, everyone came out not only satisfied by the outcome but elated by the process and by each individual's role in it.

What we project our power to be crucially impacts how we behave. Power operates through interaction between and among people at the same time that our minds recount doubts based in lived realities of the past. On guard against powerlessness, we may assume fighting mode, or we may withdraw and cede our needs. These choices are intimately influenced by the cultures in which we live. An African American woman in a mediation I mentioned earlier, finding herself racially isolated, opted to avoid meeting with her fellow leaders—a self-protective decision since her white colleagues had so little awareness of the racial and gendered dynamics she experienced so vividly. Lacking any support or allies, staying away may well have been her best option. But once she trusted the advocacy of an organized process for dialogue, she not only showed up but demonstrated a major capacity: to speak her truth. I have no doubt that dynamics of marginalization, while revealed, were not solved in one meeting. But this woman came away with an expanded sense of options, both for more voice and for more protection.

Power is an experience operating simultaneously as self-confidence, capacity for effective interaction, and assertion or welcoming of cultural uniqueness. At the same time, organizational structures importantly shape how those factors play out. Is there a formal hierarchy? Is power mystified? Often advocacy groups wish to share power and declare themselves collective. But without a full-bodied understanding of how informal power works, de facto hierarchy sets in. People find themselves punching shadows, which is to say, fighting against forces they sense but cannot name because reality is mystified by idealism. Simultaneously, the larger social structure within which all this takes place is foundational but often invisible. Where is the money? What policy decisions are impacting the organization without clear knowledge of its members? How does the central ideology of the particular society create pressures to behave in ways that diminish options?

Conflict is a petri dish for learning about all these dynamics—if people can confront it with honesty and respectful kindness. Right now, the rightward lurch in American polity demands resistance, which in turn encourages the building of solidarity across identity differences, an opportunity to practice new ways of relating with mutuality. Right along with a global economy, we live in a multicultural community. Sharing power is not something given by one person to another: a contradiction in terms. Sharing is a two-way process: In my (white) experience, I give to you and you to me. I receive as a gift what you offer while I do my best to filter what I give from remnants of any supposed superiority.

Embody Equality

"Sharing power" is where my final call to action lives. How many ways we are kept, indeed driven, apart, even while we develop methodologies intended to create unity! Emphasizing this premise is not simply a matter of values. It is imperative if we are to mobilize the solidarity needed to take power on levels of government and environment when those moments of opportunity occur.

I sometimes find myself, socks in hand, daydreaming about various ways such moments might occur. On the day I write this paragraph, I feel no certainty that electoral opportunities will occur again in the United States. The Trump rollercoaster may not tolerate any barrier on the tracks demanded by mere voters. As the electorate turns away from the strongman in office, he may well use all the powers he is currently concentrating in the presidency to bypass a possible change of government via the ballot box. Of course, that may not be our American fate. There are still multiple forms of opposition, from the courts and from many, many sectors of civil society. But I think it wise to be considering, and planning for, alternatives.

Mass demonstrations of people power are in and of themselves rarely the route to regime change. There are exceptions: the Arab Spring of 2011, a Bangladeshi youth rebellion in 2024, and so on. But even when heads of state don't topple, huge numbers of people protesting in the streets together matter. They may influence policy, protecting rights for otherwise voiceless segments of the population. More importantly, though, they encourage otherwise-privatized people to public action. That experience is not only invigorating but also educational. We learn how to organize, to march together on public streets, to have fun inventing creative slogans and images, to walk shoulder by shoulder with people we might not ever otherwise encounter. When I think of the notion of insurrectionary calisthenics, I celebrate every protest demonstration as a chance to build more muscle.

Change may be stimulated by other kinds of occurrences as well, before, during, or after mass protest. Climate disasters are already shaking the foundations of the sociopolitical order. In all the drama of headlined events such as Israeli massacres of Gazans or insane-seeming funding decisions flowing like Niagara from Washington, we forget, at our great loss, to dig into the media for news of South Saharan Africa, or South Asia, or other places where change is also dramatically afoot. What will it mean to the world order if the major provider of food internationally migrates to those places that are still primarily agriculturally based? Maintaining a closeness to nature that the "developed" world long ago abandoned, will they be our saviors? In what ways will the centers of gravity of the global economy migrate to the southern hemisphere as the climate increasingly erodes further north? We cannot know the future, of course, but it's wise to imagine unimaginable possibilities.

Meanwhile, beyond exercising our powers of vision and learning to make conflict constructive, there are many other ways to strengthen our ability to participate in progress, and, in that process, to begin right now, right here (wherever you are) to create the world we wish to live in.

Given material realities of inequality, what does it mean to practice equality on a day-to-day level? So saturated are we in the "normality" of discrimination, the very language for overcoming it conveys the opposite of what is intended. Diversity, equity, inclusion: each of these words both expands and simultaneously limits vision. Diverse from what? The notion supposes a center with "diverse" people on the margins. Consider the common sentence, "We want to include diverse people." Are the white people in the comprised group diverse? No, "diverse" implicitly means everyone who is not "white" by the definition of dominance: the "others" who may very well include people with disabilities, the elderly, and sometimes even women in general. If equality depends on mutuality, then the very concept of diversity contradicts equality.

Equity suggests a balance. I think of an old-fashioned see-saw, a child at either end, perfectly balanced in the air. Then I remember the worst fall of my own childhood. On a very long see-saw, with me at the high end, the child on the other end, much heavier than I, landed her downward swing with a bump and slid off. I fell straight down and crashed, sitting straight up, with the odd sensation of feeling nothing—everything from my head down to my toes literally numb. Gradually my body thawed, not a happy thing in one way but very relieving to the adults. X-rays, braces, and days of pain followed. I came away with the hard knowledge that there is no equitable balance as long as power is unequal.

The great weight of white privilege continually exposes people of color to disadvantage, no matter everyone's good intentions. So even while people of all races struggle in the face of hardships, true solidarity remains tenuous. We see this reality play out all the time in workplaces: who gets hired is very different from who gets promoted, treated with dignity, adequately compensated, mentored into leadership.

One example from my teaching experience at UC Berkeley: my classes on conflict resolution tended to be attended by many students of color. Was that because I had a reputation as an easy grader? (True) Or because these students were so eager to learn how to handle conflict constructively because they found themselves in quiet conflict all the time? (Also true). I was shocked one day when I asked my class the question.

"You're the only professor who ever asked me about my experiences on campus and then used the word 'racism' to label them," one person said.

"You're the only professor I've ever had a one-to-one conversation with," said another.

The white students in class were as surprised as I was. But I was also horrified and angry that the system of which I was a part recruited these students and then abandoned them to such total alienation. We had "diversity," but did we have equity?

Inclusion is even more problematic: "Why won't they come to our party?" How often white groups yearn to break through a color barrier, genuinely wanting to include absent members of the larger community in their activities. But on what terms? So normalized are dominant ways of doing things that we are not even aware that they are dominant. No longer chosen from a variety of possible approaches, these set practices exclude even while one may honestly wish for the opposite. "Our party" is a very particular party. Not only do people not of the dominant majority (in the United States now actually a minority in numbers although not in power) fail to realize how much we oppress those who regard things through a different cultural lens, but we have no idea how much we're missing! How mind blowing it can be to hear that the way we've organized our campaign is only one of many possible ways; that meetings traditionally held prisoner to agendas filled with drudgery might become fun exercises in learning and creation, if conducted differently—and get the work done even more efficiently. When I co-led a truly multicultural committee brought together to organize a conference in a way that would actually be equitable and attract the "diverse people" usually missing, the first challenge I faced was a rebellion against the timeline.

"But there is a deadline," I protested. "Several hundred people will arrive at a definite time, and we need to be ready."

Fortunately, I knew many of the people in the group well, and I loved and trusted them. We had built relationships in different places and contexts over many years. "It'll be okay," my co-chair Mary Trujillo said. I gulped and threw out the timeline. Many nights I awoke in a sweat, ledgers of money for which we were responsible swimming in my head, calendars with days crossed off looming over my head, bearing us closer and closer to opening day. I'd call Mary and say, "Tell me it'll be okay."

"It'll be okay," she'd say—and miraculously, I relaxed. In the end, it was okay. We arrived at the goal line with time to spare and put on a great conference.

To recognize control is the first step toward equal relationships; to relinquish control the second. But that's not the end of the process. The next, most crucial step is to learn mutuality. Giving up control does not mean falling silent. If my ways are not the only way, there probably is still lots that is worthwhile that I know. That is equally true for my co-madres. If I contribute my wisdom and my colleague contributes hers, together we stand to create something better than either of us knew before. That creative act of collaboration, grounded in an excitement to go beyond convention, to embrace the unknown and create something new, is an essential standpoint for engaging in genuine multiculturalism.

The point I want most to emphasize here is this: we do not yet know what truly egalitarian relationships look or feel like. So embedded are our practices and psyches in inequality that we have no baseline on which to stand. One example tells the story.

I know some couples who decided to share parenting with strict equality. They created elaborate agreements about how they would spend equal time with their about-to-be-born child. One heterosexual couple advocated not only the imagined benefits to the parents but also to the child: to have rich and loving relationships with two adults could only support this new person to grow into a well-balanced, contented adult.

Two things immediately upset their apple cart. The baby had colic. Crying often and at length in gastric distress, they could only be calmed by the breast. So biology upset social planning. Both parents had options for by-the-hour work, but he (an emergency room doctor) was paid substantially more than she (a social worker): where the majority of a workforce is female, pay is likely to be at most 80 percent of male-centered professions' rates. Anchored at home to care for their beloved but screaming infant, the mother spent less time working, the father more. As his career became more central to the family, her options for earning the money they needed grew thinner. Meanwhile, away from home and feeling incompetent to give the baby what they needed, the father became more distant. The baby bonded securely with the parent with the breasts and rejected comfort from the other one. So biology, fortune, and money-earning opportunities that had nothing intrinsically to do with the humans impacted, created an imbalance that, over time, grew greater and harder to remedy.

Although this example demonstrates some very specific conditions, the factors involved are generalizable. First, the social structures we take for granted impact us in ways that are not often obvious. Imagine a community in which many people live in collective habitats and have babies more or less at the same time. What if childcare labor is spread among many people of all genders? If one baby needs to be breastfed (my own son rejected a bottle firmly almost from day one), what if there were no proscriptions against non-bio moms nursing babies not birthed by them? In past eras, wet nursing was entirely acceptable, a common practice for upper-class people, still common among relatives and neighbors in the parts of India where I lived. But modern societies have harder boundaries against things of the body, including breastfeeding. We could belabor the example by introducing strategies for helping our young couple overcome their difficulty—baby bottles and formula and readily available expert advice about handling colic. But if we take away the main points—that the ways we live are normalized in what we assume to be possible and limited by the material prospects offered in our environments—then we can extend this example to many others.

Every experience of life is filled with lessons in accepting hierarchy. I've outlined some of this process in an earlier chapter. Isolation of children from peer packs results in sibling competitiveness and sometimes brutality. Schools use competition as motivation as well as evaluation. Gaining employment is a competitive process, as is advancing through the hierarchies that structure workplaces. The list goes on through life.

My friend Roberto often says, "Multiculturalism means learning on the job. We're all beginners." That is true and, reflecting Roberto's generosity, also not true; people long consigned to "minority" status have a lot more practice figuring out the reality of those who are dominant than the other way around. With humility and a keen ability to listen and believe, white people have much to learn from those who do not inhabit the dominant center. People of color and others accustomed to sidelining also, of course, have things to learn—and that is a tale for them to spin, not me.

I leave you with these reminders:

When you feel fearful, sad, or angry, you are not crazy. Not to feel those things in the face of the tattering of human society and the havoc we have wreaked on the earth would indeed be insane.

When you feel confused, sensing some elusive truth, you are correct. Talk to others, piece together the bits of reality you each can grasp, and insist on piercing the lies and mystification that cloud the truth from clear vision.

When you feel lonely, insecure, and overworked, know you are not alone. That is the harm imposed by the many deficiencies in the organization of modern society. When we join with others, awareness of shared reality grows in clarity, liberating agency, and aggregating power to change the world.

Notes

Chapter 1

1 Emily A. Shrider, "Poverty in the United States: 2023" (United States Census Bureau, 9/10/2024) https://www.census.gov/library/publications/2024/demo/p60-283.html.

Chapter 2

1 *Some Trouble with Cows: Making Sense of Social Conflict* (University of California Press, 1994).

2 *Bitters in the Honey: Tales of Hope and Disappointment Across Divides of Race and Time* (University of Arkansas Press, 1999).

3 *Standing on Both Feet: Voices of Older Mixed Race Americans* (Routledge, 2013).

Chapter 3

1 "Racial and Ethnic Disparities: Research and Statistics on Racial and Ethnic Disparities in the Criminal Legal System" (Prison Policy Initiative, accessed 8/29/2025) https://www.prisonpolicy.org/research/racial_and_ethnic _disparities/.

2 Timothy Shea, M.D., et al, "Racial and Ethnic Inequalities in Inpatient Psychiatric Civil Commitment" (*Psychiatric Services*, vol. 73, no. 12) https://psychiatryonline .org/doi/10.1176/appi.ps.202100342.

Chapter 5

1 Brenna Harper, "Divorce Statistics in 2025 (Latest U.S. Data)" https://mazeoflove .com/divorce/.

2 "Women's-to-men's Earnings Ratio, 197902008" (TED: The Economics Daily) https://www.bls.gov/opub/ted/2009/jul/wk4/art05.htm; https://iwpr.org/wp -content/uploads/2024/03/Occupational-Wage-Gap-2024-Fact-Sheet-1.pdf.

3 Antonio Gramsci, *The Modern Prince and Other Writings* (International Publishers, 1957); Christine Buci-Glicksmann, "Hegemony and Consent: a Political Strategy" in Anne Showstack Sassoon, *Approaches to Gramsci* (Writers and Readers Publishing Cooperative Society Ltd., 1982)

4 "Historical Households Tables" (United States Census Bureau, 11/2024) https:// www.census.gov/data/tables/time-series/demo/families/households.html; "12% of European Households have 3 or More Children" (European Large Families Confederation, 6/3/2022) https://www.elfac.org/12-of-european-households -have-3-or-more-children/#:~:text=At%2520EU%2520level%2520in%25021,with %2520children%2520in%2520those%2520countries; https://www.parents.com/ pregnancy/everything-pregnancy/why-one-and-done-families-are-on-the-rise/; https://www.bbc.com/worklife/article/20230110-only-child-or-siblings-one-and -done.

5 Katherine Schaeffer, "America's Public School Teachers are Far Less Racially and Ethnically Diverse than Their Students" (Pew Research Center, 12/10/2021).

Chapter 6

1 "Prevalence of Any Mental Disorder Among Adolescents" (National Institute of Mental Health) https://www.nimh.nih.gov/health/statistics/mental-illness#part _2632.

2 "EU comprehensive approach to mental health" (European Commission, Public Health) https://health.ec.europa.eu/non-communicable-diseases/mental-health _en.

Chapter 7

1 "Antidepressant Drugs Market Size" (Global Market Insights, Report ID: GMI2505, February 2025) https://www.gminsights.com/industry-analysis/antidepressant -drugs-market.

2 James C. Scott, *Seeing Like a State* (Veritas Paperbacks, 1999).

3 James C. Scott, *Domination and the Arts of Resistance: Hidden Transcripts* (Yale University Press, 1992).

Chapter 8

1 Christopher R. Browning, *Ordinary Men: Reserve Police Battalion 101 and the Final Solution in Poland* (HarperCollins, 1992).

Chapter 9

1 Jeffrey M. Jones, "Church Attendance Has Declined in Most U.S. Religious Groups" (Wellbeing, Gallup, 3/25/2024) https://news.gallup.com/poll/642548/church -attendance-declined-religious-groups.aspx.

2 Hattie Williams, "'Dramatic Growth' in Church Attendance by Young People, Bible Society Research Finds" (Church Times, 8/28/2025) https://www.churchtimes.co .uk/articles/2025/11-april/news/uk/dramatic-growth-in-young-people-attending -church-bible-society-research-finds.

3 Sara Diamond, "Spiritual Warfare: The Politics of the Christian Right" https:// wisconsinwatch.org/2024/10/christian-religious-right-election-trump-politics -evangelical-nationalism/.

Chapter 10

1 Carrie Spector, "70 Years after Brown v. Board of Education, New Research Shows Rise in School Segregation" (Graduate School of Education, Stanford University, 5/6/2024) https://ed.stanford.edu/news/70-years-after-brown-v-board-education -new-research-shows-rise-school-segregation.

Chapter 12

1 Arlie Hochschild, *The Second Shift: Working Parents and the Revolution at Home* (Viking Penguin, 1989).

Chapter 13

1 C. Wright Mills, *The Power Elite* (Oxford University Press, 1957).

2 "Racial and Ethnic Disparities: Research and Statistics on Racial and Ethnic Disparities in the Criminal Legal System" (Prison Policy Initiative) https://www.prisonpolicy.org/research/racial_and_ethnic_disparities/.

3 "Maternal Mortality In The U.S. Declined, Though Disparities In The Black Population Persist" (Policy Center for Maternal Mental Health) https://policycentermmh.org/maternal-mortality-in-the-u-s-a-declining-trend-with-persistent-racial-disparities-in-the-black-population/.

4 Richard Zweigenhaft, "Diversity Among Fortune 500 CEOs from 2000 to 2020: White Women, Hi-Tech South Asians, and Economically Privileged Multilingual Immigrants from Around the World (Who Rules America?)" (University of California, Santa Cruz, 1/2021) https://whorulesamerica.ucsc.edu/diversity/diversity_update_2020.html.

Chapter 14

1 https://www.pewresearch.org/politics/2024/04/09/age-generational-cohorts-and-party-identification/.

Chapter 15

1 Berthold Brecht, "To Posterity," trans. H. R. Hays, in *Selected Poems* (Grove Press, 1947).

2 John Reed, *Ten Days the Shook the World* (Boni & Liveright, 1919); Leon Trotsky, *The History of the Russian Revolution*, trans. Max Eastman (Well Red Publications, 2007); Isaac Deutscher, *The Prophet Armed: Trotsky, 1879-1921* (Oxford University Press, 1954).

3 James C. Scott, *Two Cheers for Anarchism* (Princeton University Press, 2012).

4 Beth Roy, "Talking About Power" https://www.bethroy.org/radical-therapy.

Review of Concepts

- Identity is formed on multiple levels of human consciousness, both emotional and intellectual. Gleanings of who we are lie in what we experience, what we hear from the people around us and what we observe them doing, and from impersonal media sources, including formal education.

- From the very beginning, identity becomes politicized. How we regard people with characteristics different from our own is part and parcel of how we understand power and entitlement, our own and others. We internalize institutional systems of inequality in which we live in the form of assumptions, beliefs, attitudes, and expectations. We lose a fundamental grounding in humanity: an unshakeable recognition of commonality with others and of goodness in ourselves.

- In the United States, among those internalized structures are core myths of meritocracy and individualism. We come to believe that the highest state of human development is aloneness, that anyone can achieve the American Dream through hard work and obedience, and that we are responsible for our own failures when we find ourselves falling far short of the promised marks of success.

- To abandon the Dream, however, leaves us adrift in an unbearably grim reality, so we turn to two alternative explanations for the plight in which we find ourselves: we are inadequate either in ability or psychology, or we are the victims of injustice: somebody stole my cheese!

- The first explanation produces depression and anxiety, so sufferers turn to psychotherapeutic solace. But psychiatry and its pharmaceutical sponsors compound an ideology of individualism, rendering us all the more isolated and impotent to change the damaging conditions we experience.

- The second explanation—that others benefit while we are deprived—fans flames of hateful division, again contradicting collective action that might produce collective solutions.

- And so we identify ourselves tribally, a difficult reach for members of the dominant majority who have lost a clear sense of any identity except race and nation, providing opportunity for a supreme individualist to obtain undue power by promising to solve all problems.

- Instead, all the ills of society—alienation, "mental health" malaise, racism, sexism, anti-LGBTQ prejudice, and more—are intensified.

The Making of a Radical

I graduated college disappointed that all the erudition of my professors had not come even close to answering the questions that seemed to me most urgent—the same questions SY laid out so many years later. Determined to travel somewhere in the world where I might experience very different ways of thinking and understanding the world, to escape the confining conceptual boundaries within which I knew myself—and us all—to be imprisoned, I landed in New York on the first lap of a journey concocted by some of those same professors. Almost immediately, in this heartland of American capitalism, I found a perspective that placed everything else I was to learn in a compelling framework. I was drawn to several very different people who were Marxists. The first I married, the second opened to me communities that welcomed and transformed me, and the third remains a simple voice of wisdom, radicalism, and kindness that rekindles optimism every time it flags.

I mentioned in an earlier chapter but didn't properly introduce Probhat. As college graduation drew near, all I knew I wanted to do was live in a culture so different from everything I'd known that I would be able to see reality from the other side of the mirror. Three of my professors listened to my quest and were inspired to help me on my way. One of them taught part-time at the New School for Social Research in Manhattan. I knew of the New School as an exciting community of progressive thinkers. The New School sheltered many Jewish scholars from Europe who had fled the Nazi regime. Disappointed that I had missed Herbert Marcuse's active presence on the Brandeis faculty, I now looked eagerly forward to encountering some of his peers in New York. But that was not why my mentors wanted to send me there. I had my eye on Burma as the "other side of the mirror." Unfortunately for me, though, Burma had recently closed its borders to Europeans, seeking to sever colonialist ties. So one of my sponsors came up with a plan to get me into Burma by way of a teaching gig in an East African university, where he knew numbers of Burmese students were enrolled. To do that, I'd need at least a master's degree, something he believed I could earn quickly at the New School. So he used his sociology connections to get me admitted.

In my first semester, I enrolled in a class called "Social Development in a Global Context." Taught by a Swedish elder, I thought it likely to orient me in useful ways to one aspect of where I was headed. But I found the class to be dry to the point of boredom—until one dashing student from India asked a question that livened things up. The professor had listed many theories of economic development, only to dismiss each with a one-sentence critique. Probhat raised his hand and asked, "If you don't hold with any of these theories, how do you think economic development does happen?" The professor repeated his recitation, unaltered.

At length he paused and Probhat raised his hand again. "You've dismissed all these theories; what is *your* theory of development?"

We all groaned as a third listing of debunked ideas began. Thankfully, the bell rang to end the class session, and we all streamed out.

Soon crowded in an elevator with fellow students, I spotted Probhat and thanked him for his questions. I asked, "Did he ever actually answer them? What did I miss?"

He looked at me keenly and said, "Want to get some coffee?"

Two weeks later we—free thinkers, rebels against conventional matrimony, actual and would-be culture travelers—stood before a judge and married, our decision an act of self-defense against the uproar our relationship caused in both our worlds.

For all our differences, my parallels with Probhat were stark. He came to the United States ostensibly as a graduate student, but actually to escape the disappointments of newly independent India. From his teen years, he had joined the anti-colonial movement, engaging in actions both legal and not. Throughout the movement, he avoided capture by imperial forces, but one of the first acts of the post-empire government led by Jawaharlal Nehru was to imprison many of the young firebrands who had been so instrumental in freeing the land from British rule. However crucial their rebellious acumen had been before liberation, it was considerably less welcome now. In prison for a year, held without charge or trial, these young activists did what young activists do: they read revolutionary literature, especially studying Marxism. In long hot evenings of discussion and debate, they acquired identities as communists.

Probhat studied history in detail, South Asian history of course, but also the history of capitalism. I longed for a narrative that made sense of things, and he offered exactly that. His accounts of the great sweep of changes that resulted in the society we now knew compelled me. He presented Marxism to me, a gift to his new bride, quite literally in the form of a copy of *Das Kapital*. Marx's monumental analysis of economic value, a detailed unpacking of relationships, deeply appealed both to my mathematical sensibilities and to my longing to name the complex realities swirling around us.

Even more, Probhat introduced me to people who moved me deeply. Paul Alexander, his closest friend, was a child of the Depression. Twenty years my senior, reared on a dusty farm in Oklahoma, veteran of the Second World War, in 1962 when I met him in New York City Paul was married to Pat, a British playwright, and raising a lively four-year-old named Hailey. Working as a truck driver, he had long since joined the Communist Party of America. Once landed in New York, Probhat had headed to the CPUSA offices, the only place he could think of where he might make human connections. There he met Paul, and they immediately clicked: a tall, lanky farm boy and autodidact from Oklahoma and an emotionally wrought, half-starved revolutionary ten years his junior just off the boat (literally) from India.

In my memory, it was only days after we met that Probhat took me to meet Paul. We sat in the living room of the apartment he shared with his wife and daughter in Manhattan, drinking coffee and chatting. In a conversational pause, Paul looked around the room and mused, "Why do this collection of people from so many places fit so easily together?" he asked, listing all our diverse origins. I shyly waited for him to answer his own question, knowing that he was speaking directly to me. "How odd and wonderful," he went on, "that we come from so many different corners of the world, all inspired by a revolution that happened somewhere none of us has ever been. The ideal of revolution is what binds us, whatever our disappointments in what exists so far: the ideal of a just society."

Today, I am certainly less starry-eyed, not prepared to wait for the revolution. But I went on to learn a great deal both about Marx's theory of how history moves from one form of social organization to another, and also about the reasons for the failures of the revolutionary experiments we've so far known. Improbably, my encounters with Marxism entwine deeply with my later counseling and conflict transformation work. The bridge between theory and practice is the third person I mentioned encountering in New York.

I've said that my first experience of organizing in Fort Worth took place as part of a committee trying to prepare the city to desegregate schools in 1954. The heart and leadership of that group came from a woman who worked for the American Friends Service Committee, the action arm of the Quaker community. At this same time or a little earlier, my later friend Becky attended a summer camp sponsored by AFSC, a place where teenagers gathered to be immersed in the intercultural, peace movement-oriented values and practices of the Quakers. In our early adulthood, launched but not yet anchored, both Becky and I turned to AFSC as a welcome port. Though based in Philadelphia, the organization had a small office in Manhattan. I was hired to assist the youth director and Becky to run their switchboard, one of those that appears in old movies from time to time: a maze of wires crisscrossing each other to plug people into their calls—or in Becky's case somebody's calls. The chaos of her technical malpractices contributed much hilarity in the office, as well as some meaningful but unexpected acquaintances.

Becky and I were instant friends. She had come to New York from San Francisco to dance but joined the Quakers in disappointment. Talented modern dancer though she was, the professional dance world was not ready to embrace a woman of her size. As she nursed wounds and considered next steps, she merrily plugged people into the wrong phone calls and joined with me to organize suburban teens into peace clubs. In one community, we found intense strife between Jewish and immigrant Polish youths rendered idealistic peace work insane. So knowing nothing about how to do it except what the kids and our instincts suggested, we plunged in and organized a mediation, bringing both sides together in a high-risk meeting despite adult terror and ending with a lot more understanding and sympathy among the kids. Our otherwise kind but now alarmed bosses at AFSC promptly fired both Becky and me.

Becky was from San Francisco and a red-diaper baby, meaning that she was the daughter of communists. She had grown up with the FBI at the door of her home, in the terrifying shadow of the execution of Ethel and Julius Rosenberg, party members accused of revealing nuclear secrets to the Soviets. By this time, the Khrushchev Report had been released confirming what had until then been only rumored atrocities by Stalin. Becky's parents, along with many others, resigned from the party. Her Russian Jewish father was a longshoreman, a self-taught historian, art, and opera lover. The stepmother who mostly raised her wrote and taught poetry. These charismatic, talented people became my second family. In these early days, Probhat, Becky, and I spent a lot of time in a bar called Chumley's while they debated intricacies of Marxist theory and strategy, and I soaked it all up. More important than anything they argued over, though, is the framework in which their differences nested: faith in progress and especially a conviction that a better form of society could be imagined and built.

That vision is one underlying all my face-to-face work. Again and again, I ask myself—and often my clients—what would be different about this picture if we lived in a just society? In that world, how clear it would be that the problems you suffer are not your individual fault but imposed by the deficiencies in our shared system. And that is the essence of radicalism: always looking beyond the given to the just and the humane.

Bibliography

Allison, Dorothy. *Two or Three Things I Know for Sure*. Penguin Books, 1995.

Arendt, Hannah. *Eichmann in Jerusalem: A Report on the Banality of Evil*. The Viking Press, 1963.

Baldwin, James. "Fifth Avenue, Uptown." *Esquire*, October 16, 2007.

Baldwin, James. *Notes of a Native Son*. The Modern Library, 1955.

Brecht, Bertolt. "To Posterity." Translated by H. R. Hays. In *Selected Poems*. Grove Press, 1947.

Browning, Christopher R. *Ordinary Men: Reserve Police Battalion 101 and the Final Solution in Poland*. HarperCollins, 1992.

Buci-Glicksmann, C. "Hegemony and Consent: A Political Strategy." In Anne Showstack Sassoon, *Approaches to Gramsci*. Writers and Readers Publishing Cooperative Society Ltd., 1982.

Coates, Te-Nehisi. *Between the World and Me*. Spiegel Grau. 2015.

Deutscher, Isaac. *The Prophet Armed: Trotsky, 1879-1921*. Oxford University Press, 1954.

Diamon, Sara. "Spiritual Warfare: The Politics of the Christian Right." *Wisconsin Watch*, 2025.

Gramsci, Antonio. *The Modern Prince and Other Writings*. International Publishers, 1957.

Harper, Brenna. "Divorce Statistics in 2025." *Maze of Love, Latest U.S. Data*, 2025.

Hochschild, Arlie. *The Second Shift: Working Parents and the Revolution at Home*. Viking Penguin, 1989.

Jones, Jeffrey M. "Church Attendance Has Declined in Most U.S. Religious Groups." *Wellbeing, Gallup*, 3/25/2024.

Mills, C. Wright. *The Power Elite*. Oxford University Press, 1957.

Reed, John. *Ten Days that Shook the World*. Boni & Liveright, 1919.

Roy, Beth. *Bitters in the Honey: Tales of Hope and Disappointment Across Divides of Race and Time*. University of Arkansas Press, 1999.

Roy, Beth. *Some Trouble with Cows: Making Sense of Social Conflict*. University of California Press, 1994.

Schaeffer, Katherine. "America's Public School Teachers are Far Less Racially and Ethnically Diverse than Their Students." Pew Research Center, 12/10/2021.

Scott, James C. *Domination and the Arts of Resistance: Hidden Transcripts*. Yale University Press, 1992.

Scott, James C. *Seeing Like a State: How Certain Schemes to Improve the Human Condition Have Failed*. Veritas Paperbacks, 1999.

Scott, James C. *Two Cheers for Anarchism*. Princeton University Press, 2012.

Shea, Timothy, M.D., et al. "Racial and Ethnic Inequalities in Inpatient Psychiatric Civil Commitment." *Psychiatric Services*, vol. 73, no. 12, 2022, 1322–9.

Shrider, Emily A. "Poverty in the United States: 2023." United States Census Bureau, 2024.

Spector, Carrie. "Spiritual Warfare: The Politics of the Christian Right." Graduate School of Education, Stanford University, 5/6/2024.

Toshiro, Cathy. *Standing on Both Feet: Stories of Older Mixed Race Americans*. Routledge, 2013.

Trotsky, Leon. *The History of the Russian Revolution*. Translated by Max Eastman. Well Red Publications, 2007.

Trujillo, Mary Adams, S. Y. Bowland, Linda James Myers, Phillip M. Richards, and Beth Roy, eds. *Re-Centering Culture and Knowledge in Conflict Resolution Practice*. Syracuse University Press, 2008.

Wilkerson, Isabel. *The Warmth of Other Suns: The Epic Story of America's Great Migration*. Vintage Books. 2011.

Williams, Hattie. "'Dramatic Growth' in Church Attendance by Young People, Bible Society Research Finds." *Church Times*, 8/28/2025.

Williams, Patricia J. *The Alchemy of Race and Rights*. Harvard University Press, 1991.

Zweigenhaft, Richard. "Diversity Among Fortune 500 CEOs from 2000 to 2020: White Women, Hi-Tech South Asians, and Economically Privileged Multilingual Immigrants from Around the World (*Who Rules America?*)." University of California, Santa Cruz, 2021.

Index

About the Author

Beth Roy, PhD, with a long career as a conflict mediator and scholar of identity-based social divisions, draws on stories from her practice and research, as well as from her own life, to look deeply into moments of historic conflict. The author of *Some Trouble with Cows: Making Sense of Social Conflict* among other volumes, Dr. Roy taught peace and conflict studies at UC Berkeley and co-founded the Practitioners Research and Scholarship Institute, as well as co-editing two anthologies of writings on race and professional practice.